57 YEARS

A HISTORY OF THE FREEDOM SUITS IN THE MISSOURI COURTS

Anthony J. Sestric

REEDY PRESS
St. Louis, Missouri

Reedy Press
PO Box 5131
St. Louis, MO 63139, USA

Library of Congress Control Number: 2012931389

ISBN: 978-1-935806-24-0

Please visit our website at www.reedypress.com.

Cover design by Jill Halpin

Printed in the United States of America
12 13 14 15 16   5 4 3 2 1

CONTENTS

ACKNOWLEDGMENTS

I WOULD LOVE TO TAKE FULL CREDIT FOR THIS BOOK, BUT TRUTH AND honesty will not allow it. There are several people who deserve much of the credit for whatever you may find of value or interest in these pages.

First and foremost is Jenna Kopff, my paralegal, research assistant, proofreader, driver, and the most valuable contributor to this project. Without her, this book would never have been published.

Next were the efforts of Mariano Favazza, the former St. Louis City circuit clerk, who discovered the "freedom suits" in the archives of the clerk's office. Mariano was the driving force behind collecting and preserving these documents and getting them to the Missouri State Archives, part of the office of Secretary of State Robin Carnahan. Secretary Carnahan caused the records to be indexed, preserved, digitalized, and made available to the public.

Mr. Michael Everman, CA, the archivist of the Local Records Program for the secretary of state's office at the Missouri State Archives–St. Louis was the epitome of the researcher's dream. Mr. Everman was so encouraging and helpful in finding the originals of the freedom-suit records, and leading us to a wealth of additional source documents, that we felt, at times, as if we were overburdening him. He deserves more special thanks and acknowledgments than I can offer.

Since the St. Louis Public Library stacks and research facilities were unavailable due to renovation of the main library, we turned to its counterpart, the St. Louis County Library. Through a cooperative agreement between the city and county libraries, we were able to find materials available only through the library's collection. The staff at the main branch on Lindbergh was as helpful, patient, and kind as if we were major benefactors to the library. We shall be forever grateful.

Last, and by no means least, many thanks to the American Culture Studies Program in Arts & Sciences at Washington University for putting online the digitalized summary of the freedom suits.

INTRODUCTION

AMERICA IS "CELEBRATING" THE 150TH ANNIVERSARY OF THE CIVIL WAR. The debate still goes on as to the causes of the war, but in the end it was the war to end slavery in the United States.

At the time of the Louisiana Purchase, there were few laws in the United States concerning slavery. The decision to restrict or permit slavery in what would become the state of Missouri was made partly by early inhabitants of the territory and partly by others. The story of Missouri's struggle to come to terms with slavery is unique because of the state's distinct geographic and cultural diversity.

This is the story of what took place between 1803 and 1861 in Missouri, with events controlled by Missourians. To some extent, the story extended beyond the beginning of the war. The lives of many of the people went on beyond the war, and the whole story needs to be told. It is also a story of what might have happened in 1861 had only a few events changed. The Civil War might not have taken place. Persons of mixed color might never have been enslaved. Dred Scott might have remained free. Not many people know that the Scott decision reversed forty years of Missouri precedent, and it was the election of judges from rural Missouri that kept Dred and Harriet's case from being only one of some three hundred cases in which slaves were freed.

This book is my humble attempt to describe the courage, bravery, heroism, and fortitude of the people of Missouri to limit and overcome the horrors of slavery and to keep Missouri in the Union. It tells of the lawyers and judges who shaped the history of Missouri and the United States both in the freedom suits and in their work in government, politics, and business. Some acquired incredible wealth, but most did not. Some risked their lives to preserve the Union. The dramatic stories of some of these men are worthy of film, so filled are they with courage, love, devotion, greed, success, and sadness. These stories also demonstrate how the practice of law has changed and how the divided culture of Missouri—the rural versus urban split—is a residue of the earliest history of the state.

This book is also about the bravery and courage of the more than four hundred slaves who fought for their freedom. The filing of the early freedom suits resulted, often, in plaintiffs being "sold down the river," sold to masters down the Mississippi, never to be seen again. Once the judges and plaintiffs' lawyers figured out how to stop these sales, the slaves were incarcerated until their trial. But this often resulted in the slaves being "hired out" by the sheriff, frequently leading to cruel treatment, as bad as that handed out by their master. Finally, the courts required the masters to post a bond to keep possession of their slaves. The bonds were normally high enough that masters would make sure the slaves were present when their day in court came, lest the masters forfeit a huge bond. But as Sancho Panza said in *Man of La Mancha*, "whether the rock hits the pot, or the pot hits the rock, it is bad for the pot." Filing for their freedom required incredible patience, courage, and an acceptance of a long and frequently discouraging process on the part of the slave.

In gathering stories about the people in this book, I wondered what might have happened in Missouri and in the country if some of the events had been slightly altered. For instance, if Edward Bates had won the Republican nomination for president in 1860 instead of Abraham Lincoln, would the Southern states have seceded? Would slavery still have been abolished? If William Scott and Priestly McBride had not been elected to replace George Tompkins and Matthias McGirk in the Missouri Supreme Court, the final result of the Dred Scott case would have led to Dred Scott being freed. If Joshua Barton had not been killed in a duel on Bloody Island, would Edward Bates have undertaken his fight for the end of slavery?

I discuss lawyers and judges first, not because their efforts were more courageous or significant than those of their clients, but merely because a description of the lives and personalities of the players aids in our understanding of the dynamics of the freedom suits.

As a full discussion of the hundreds of freedom suits filed in Missouri would produce an encyclopedic tome, I have chosen thirteen for the purposes of this book.

57 YEARS

TERRITORIAL LAWS

THE LOUISIANA TERRITORY, ESTABLISHED IN 1804, WAS GOVERNED BY A president-appointed territorial governor. Initially, the Louisiana Territory included all of the Louisiana Purchase. Soon, however, the property was divided, with New Orleans, the prize of the purchase, being set apart. By 1812, the Missouri Territory was established as part of the Upper Louisiana Territory, and was also governed by presidential appointment.[1]

President Thomas Jefferson originally appointed W. C. Claiborne to assume the civil duties of the territory and James Wilkinson to assume its military duties. Claiborne and Wilkinson then appointed Amos Stoddard as governor.[2]

Laws regarding slaves in the Missouri Territory proved complex and in some instances inconsistent. Stoddard blended existing Spanish law with what was necessary from American law. Stoddard reappointed many Spanish officials to continue the day-to-day operations of the territorial government, although Spanish soldiers were limited in their power. Because much of the land consisted of old Spanish land grants, early territorial government was a mix of old Spanish law, the common law of England, a little bit of French civil law, and a hodgepodge of additional laws necessitated by the circumstances of the day.[3]

To add to this cultural stew, linguistically, the Missouri Territory was dominated by the French. Most slaves spoke French, and to a certain extent Creole,[4] and as late as 1818, two-thirds of the white population of St. Louis spoke predominantly French.[5] So there were old Spanish land grants, Spanish laws on slavery, French spoken by the slaves and most of their masters, and finally laws and customs (some of which were ignored) necessitated by tradition and practicality in the new West.

The court system of the Missouri Territory was established by the federal government in 1812. The supreme court consisted of three judges appointed for four-year terms, any two of which could conduct business, along with other lower courts, including justices of the peace. For the first eight years of territorial law, the legislative functions in Missouri were performed by the governor, the three supreme court judges, and after 1812, a bicameral legislature.

From the very beginning, territorial law acknowledged the right of "Negroes" to seek their freedom in the territorial courts. Many of the free blacks were the poorest of the poor, and were unable to pay even the modest filing fees. The 1807 statutes provided for slaves to sue as poor persons.

The full territorial laws are printed at the end of this section. The territorial laws were adopted by the territorial governor in 1807, since Missouri was not yet a state. The concept of allowing blacks to sue for their freedom was relatively common throughout the rest of the nation, but throughout the Southern states, these laws were a measure to protect freed blacks, more so than a devise to allow slaves to gain their freedom. A part of the statutory scheme was a provision that to enslave a freed slave was a capital offense. The 1807 statutes were effectively repealed with the 1824 statutes, which was adopted by the Missouri Legislature after Missouri was admitted as a state.

The 1824 statutes expanded the grounds and the basis for the filing of the freedom suits. With statehood, Missouri became a "slave state," but the antislavery soul of many Missourians remained. There was a division between an antislavery St. Louis and the rest of the state, which favored slavery. The 1824 statute was ultimately abrogated with the end of the Civil War and the adoption of the 13th and 14th amendments to the United States Constitution.

For instance, enslaving a freed person was punishable by death "without the benefit of clergy." Stealing someone else's slave was similarly punishable by death "without the benefit of clergy." It was permissible to free your slaves in your last will and testament. But if the slaves were not of sound mind and body, or were over the age of forty-five, or were male and under twenty-one or female and under eighteen, the former owner's estate was responsible for maintaining the freed slaves.

No one should ever assume that Missouri "slave laws" were particularly enlightened. Many of the statutes entitling slaves to sue for freedom were modeled after some of the earlier Southern state laws designed to ensure that emancipated slaves were not re-enslaved. Missouri had an interesting combination of laws allowing freedom suits to be brought, but also contained extraordinarily harsh punishment. For instance, it was a capital offense to kill a slave, resulting in execution "without benefit of clergy" of the slave's murderer. A slave who killed his master suffered the same punishment, as did anyone convicted of the stealing or selling of any free person as a slave.

Many of the slave owners believed the slaves, because of their African heritage, had some special and secret knowledge about the healing effect of herbs and medicines. The slaves were, somewhat regularly, sought out to cure illnesses both of the masters and of other slaves. But to be sure that slaves were not going around poisoning all of the masters, slaves were only allowed to administer medicines with the consent of their owners.

Slaves were not allowed to own or carry guns, and freed slaves were only allowed one weapon. Slaves were not permitted to leave the plantation without a pass and could not visit other plantations without a pass. Any slave owner who allowed someone else's slaves to remain on his plantation without a pass for more than four hours was fined three dollars. If any slave owner allowed his slave to hire himself out, the sheriff would have arrested the slave, put the slave in jail, and after twenty days sell the slave for "ready money." Under the 1804 Louisiana Terriotorial Laws, of the sale price, 25 percent was kept to reduce the district taxes, 5 percent was paid to the sheriff "for his trouble, and the jailor's fee," and the rest paid to the former owner of the slave.

Despite severe restrictions on the travel of slaves in Missouri, travel restrictions were frequently ignored in St. Louis where communication with people off the plantation was accepted. It was quite common for slaves to travel about the area on business of their own. In this way, information about events in the community became quickly known. In this sense, enforcement of many of the slave laws was "winked at" by whites.

LAWS OF THE TERRITORY
OF LOUISIANA

AN ACT TO ENABLE PERSONS HELD IN SLAVERY, TO SUE FOR THEIR FREEDOM.*

1. Persons held in slavery to sue as paupers, when.

2. Suits, how instituted—counsel assigned petitioner—petitioner not to be removed.

3. Petitioner about to be removed, defendant may be required to enter into recognizance; petitioner may be hired out when—person hiring to enter into recognizance.

4. Weight of proof on petitioner—judgment.

5. Appeal to general court.

Be it enacted by the Legislature of the territory of Louisiana [as follows]:

1. It shall be lawful for any person held in slavery to petition the general court or any court of common pleas, praying that such person may be permitted to sue as a poor person, and stating the grounds on which the claim to freedom is founded. If in the opinion of the court the petition contains sufficient matter to authorize their interference the court shall award the necessary process to bring the cause before them.

2. The court to whom application is thus made, may direct an action of assault and battery, and false imprisonment, to be instituted in the name of the person claiming freedom against the person who claims the petitioner as a slave, to be conducted as

*Repealed R.L. 1825, p. 500, sec. 13, by the passage of the 1824 state statute expanding the scope of the freedom suits.

suits of the like nature between other persons. And the court shall assign the petitioner counsel, and if they deem it proper shall make an order directing the defendant or defendants to permit the petitioner to have a reasonable liberty of attending his counsel, and the court when occasion may require it, and that the petitioner shall not be taken nor removed out of the jurisdiction of the courts, nor be subjected to any severity because of his or her application for freedom.

3. If the court, or any judge thereof in vacation shall have reason to believe that the above order has been or is about to be violated, in such case the said court, or any judge thereof in vacation, may require that the person of the petitioner be brought before him or them, by writ of habeas corpus, and shall cause the defendant or defendants, his, her, or their agent, to enter into recognizance with sufficient security, conditioned as recited in the above order, or in case of refusal to direct the sheriff of the district to take possession of the petitioner, and hire him or her to the best advantage, which hire shall be appropriated either to the petitioner, or to the defendant or defendants, as the event of the suit may justify. And the person hiring the petitioner shall enter into recognizance with sufficient security, conditioned as the above order directs.

4. The court before whom such suit may be tried, may instruct the jury that the weight of proof lies on the petitioner, but to have regard not only to the written evidences of the claim to freedom, but to such other proofs either at law or in equity as the very right and justice of the case may require. And the court on a verdict in favor of the petitioner, may pronounce a judgment of liberation from the defendant or defendants, and all persons claiming by, from, or under, him, her, or them.

5. Suits instituted in any court of common pleas under this law, may be removed into the general court before judgment, or if judgment is given in any such cause in the court of common pleas, appeal, or writ of error shall lie to the general court as in other cases.

The foregoing is hereby declared to be a law for the territory of Louisiana, to take effect and be in force from and after the passage thereof.

June 27, 1807.

LAWS OF THE STATE OF MISSOURI
1824

AN ACT TO ENABLE PERSONS HELD IN SLAVERY TO SUE FOR THEIR FREEDOM.

Sec 1. Be it enacted by the General Assembly of the state of Missouri, That it shall be lawful for any person held in slavery to petition the circuit court, or the judge thereof in vacation, praying that such person may be permitted to sue as a poor person, and stating the ground upon which his or her claim to freedom is founded; and if, in the opinion of the court or judge, the petition contains sufficient matter to authorize the commence of a suit, such court or judge may make an order that such person be permitted to sue as a poor person to establish his or her freedom, and assign the petitioner counsel, which order shall be endorsed on the petition. And the court or judge shall, moreover, make an order that the petitioner have reasonable liberty to attend his or her counsel and the court, when occasion may require; and that the petitioner shall not be taken or removed out of the jurisdiction of the court, nor be subject to any severity because of his or her application for freedom, which order, if made in vacation, shall be endorsed on the petition, and a copy thereof endorsed on the writ and served on the defendant.

Sec 2. Be it further enacted, That if the court, or the judge thereof in vacation, shall be satisfied, at the time of the presenting the petition, or at any time during the pendency of any suit instituted under the provisions of this act, that any petitioner hath been or is about to be restrained by any person from reasonable liberty of attending his or her counsel or the court, or that the petitioner is about to be removed out of the jurisdiction of the court, or that he or she hath been or is about to be subjected to any severity because of his or her application for freedom, or that any order made by the court or judge in the premises as aforesaid has been or is about to be violated, then and in every such case, the court, or the judge thereof in vacation, may cause the petitioner to be brought before him or them by a writ of habeas corpus; and shall cause the defendant, or the person in whose possession the petitioner may be found, his or their agent, to enter into a recognizance, with a sufficient security, conditioned that the petitioner shall at all time during the pendency of the suit have reasonable liberty of attending his or her counsel, and that such petitioner shall not be removed out of the jurisdiction of the court wherein the action is to be brought or is pending, and that he or she shall not be subjected to any severity because of his or her application for freedom, which recognizance shall be recorded and filed among the records of the court, and be deemed and taken to all intents and purposes to be a record of such court. But if the party required to enter into a recognizance as aforesaid shall refuse so to do, the court or judge shall make an order that the sheriff take possession of the petitioner and hire him or her out to the best advantage, from time to time, during the pendency of the suit; and that he take a bond from the person hiring the petitioner, in such penalty as the court shall in such order direct, and with such security as the sheriff shall approve, conditioned as directed in the recognizance of the defendant, and moreover that he will pay the hire to the sheriff at the time stipulated, and return the petitioner at the end of the time for which he or she is hired, or sooner if the action shall sooner be determined; and the sheriff shall proceed accordingly, and pay the money received for hire to the party in whose favor the suit shall be determined.

Sec. 3. Be it further enacted, That all actions to be commenced and prosecuted under the provisions of this act, shall be in form, trespass, assault and battery, and false imprisonment, in the name of the petitioner, against the person holding him or her in slavery, or claiming him or her as a slave. And whenever any court of judge shall make an order as aforesaid, permitting any such suit to be brought, the clerk shall issue the necessary process, without charge to the petitioner: the declaration shall be in the common form of a declaration for assault and battery and false imprisonment, except that the plaintiff shall aver that before and at the time of the committing the grievances he or she was and still is a free person, and that the defendant held and detained him or her and still holds and detains in slavery, upon which declaration the plaintiff may give in evidence any special matter; and the defendant may plead as many pleas as he may think is necessary for his defense, or he may plead the general issue, and give the special matters in evidence. And such actions shall be conducted in other respects in the same manner as the like actions between other persons, and the plaintiff may recover damages as in other cases.

Sec. 4. Be it further enacted, That in all actions instituted under the provisions of this act, the petitioner, if he or she be a Negro or mulatto, shall be held and required to prove his or her right to freedom; but regard shall be had not only to the written evidence of his or her claim to freedom, but to such other proofs, either at law or in equity, as the very right and justice of the case may require. And if the issue be determined in favor of the petitioner, the court shall render a judgment of liberation from the defendant or defendants, and all persons claiming from, through or under him, her or them.

Sec. 5. Be it further enacted, That if any party to a suit instituted under the provisions of this act, shall feel him or herself aggrieved by the judgment of the circuit court, he or she may have and prosecute an appeal or writ of error to the supreme court, as in other cases; Provided, That if the petitioner appeal or prosecute a writ of error, he or she shall not be required to enter into a recognizance, but such appeal or writ of error shall operate as a supersedeas without such recognizance.

This act shall take effect and be in force from and after the fourth day of July next.

Approved, December 30, 1824.

The Lawyers

LOOKING BACK OVER THE EARLY HISTORY OF THE LOUISIANA TERRITORY, and more particularly the Missouri Territory, a very significant and important group was the small band of lawyers practicing in St. Louis from 1804 to 1860. The number of lawyers living in the area was only twenty in 1836, but it had grown to 367 by the beginning of the Civil War.[6] Many of them were judges, prosecutors, and government officials. The density of lawyers amounted to fewer than two per 1,000 people in 1851, compared to one per 265 people today.[7] Edward Bates was among this small band of St. Louis lawyers. Bates, attorney general of the United States under Abraham Lincoln, was one of the people who kept Missouri in the Union during the Civil War.

What attracted these lawyers to St. Louis? They came to Missouri for a variety of reasons. One was fleeing scandal in New York, another came by invitation. None of them accumulated great wealth from the practice of law, although some of them died quite wealthy because of their other investments. Some were elected or appointed to public office. A few were viewed as such scholars and teachers that lawyers would come to St. Louis for the sole purpose of studying law under their tutelage. Some published newspapers that led to the great debates in Missouri before the Civil War and pointed out the social and political competition between the urban and rural areas of Missouri, a competition which exists to this day. If they were alive today, some of them would be considered great civil rights lawyers, since they took on the rich and powerful to fight for such things as the freedom for slaves in our courts. Some were assassinated because of their legal work while others died fighting duels arising out of perceived attacks on their honor. Being a lawyer in St. Louis in the first half of the nineteenth century was a dangerous occupation, but without their presence and participation in the history of Missouri, most assuredly, Missouri, and perhaps the entire country, would look significantly different from what it does today.

One of the most disappointing aspects of their contributions to our state and our country is that none of them, except for Bates, are remembered, aside from the names of a few streets in St. Louis. Bates faired better only because of the existence of a statue of him near the northwest corner of Forest Park, bordering the Probstein Golf Course. The statue was originally intended to be installed in Lafayette Park, but a dispute concerning the paying of the sculptor resulted in the statue not being installed at all. The Forest Park commissioners paid the sculptor's fee and brought the piece to Forest Park. It was originally dedicated in 1876 at the creation of Forest Park and was installed at the southeast corner. But the statue was moved when the Missouri Department of Transportation took part of the park for the construction of Highway 40.[8]

St. Louis lawyers in the first half of the nineteenth century were influential not only because they were good lawyers, but because they were involved in so much of St. Louis society. They owned newspapers, banks, ran for public office, and also tried lawsuits. Joseph Charless, for instance, operated the *Missouri Gazette* and was one of the founders of the Bank of St. Louis, while his political opposition, Thomas Hart Benton, operated the

Enquirer and was one of the founders of the Bank of Missouri. Both ran for various offices, occasionally against each other.

During the 1830s, the readers had a choice of fourteen newspapers. Some of them, like the *Anzeiger des Westens* and the *Anzeiger des Westens–Wochenblatt* were German-language papers. Even with this seemingly limited readership, these papers lasted until the beginning of the 1900s. Of the other twelve, five—the *Daily Missouri Republican*, the *Missouri Democrat*, the *Missouri Republican*, and the *Old School Democrat*—had some permanence, although they were either bought up by or merged with other papers. For instance, the *Daily Democrat* eventually morphed into the *Globe-Democrat* after merging with the *St. Louis Globe*. Today's *St. Louis Post-Dispatch* was the result of Joseph Pulitzer's purchase of the *Westliche Post* and the *St. Louis Dispatch* in 1878, and renaming the paper the *St. Louis Post and Dispatch*, later shortened to the *St. Louis Post-Dispatch*.

The personal views of lawyers involved in freedom suits were as conflicted as the views of the population in the state. Looking at the personal and professional lives of these lawyers doesn't necessarily give us an understanding of why they would represent one side or the other in freedom suits.

The number of lawyers representing plaintiffs in freedom suits was few compared to the number of members in the bar. In some instances, lawyers would represent both plaintiffs and defendants in separate cases. For example, Joshua Barton represented the defendant, Barnabas Harris, in *Jack v. Harris*, Mathias Rose in *Winny v. Rose*, and Auguste Chouteau in *Marie v. Chouteau*. During the same period, he represented a significant number of plaintiffs, perhaps most notably slave Winny in *Winny v. Whitesides*, along with Sarah in *Sarah v. Mitchell Hatton*. When Barton represented plaintiffs, he usually partnered with lawyer Henry Geyer.

St. Louis lawyers were not universally praised for their efforts to free slaves. Reminiscent of today's claim that plaintiff lawyers sue for profit, filing baseless suits, the local press in the early 1800s muttered similar accusations. Proslavery St. Louis claimed St. Louis lawyers, hungry for business, were abusing the right to sue for their own personal gain and that the "liberty of suing for freedom has become abused by the left-handed profiteering lawyers" who encourage slaves to tell their friends, who then go back to the first lawyer, and so forth.[9] Perhaps the accusations rendered against today's plaintiffs bar sound a bit familiar. In the 1800s, it was the proslavery lobby. Today it's the pro-business lobby. We do know that at least some of these suits were financed by the white citizens of the Carondelet area.[10] Roswell Field, best known as the father of Eugene Field and one of the lawyers for Dred and Harriet Scott, and Henry T. Blow, the father of Susan Blow, were listed as some of the financiers by Albert Jefferson in his "A Heritage Remembered."[11]

Whites in Carondelet were a source of real assistance to the African-American community almost from the start of the village. In fact, Henry Blow donated the land for the first African-American church in Carondelet, and he donated the land for Public School No. 6 (later Delaney School), the first community school for African-Americans. The white churches in Carondelet raised money to stop lenders from foreclosing on the Corinthian Missionary Baptist Church at 6326 Colorado Avenue. There had always been a significant African-American community in Carondelet.[12] Interestingly, the Blow families were the original owners of Dred Scott, when they brought him to Missouri. When Dred and Harriet began their fight for freedom, the next generation of Blows financed the Scotts' litigation, and ultimately arranged for Dred and Harriet's emancipation.

Joshua Barton

Joshua Barton and his older brother David were two of ten children born to "poor but respectable parentage"—Reverend Isaac Barton and Kaziah Murphy in Greene County, Tennessee. David was born in 1783 while Joshua was born nine years later in July 1792. Both parents outlived Joshua, the reverend dying in 1846, a year after Kaziah died. Neither Joshua nor David married or left family to give any information as to exactly when they were born or significant details about their childhood. David came to Missouri first, and Joshua followed him in 1809. Joshua was yet another of the upcoming lawyers who read law under Rufus Easton. Both brothers were admitted to the bar. Joshua was considered to have one of the best legal minds in the St. Louis Bar.[13] He represented both sides in freedom suits, representing Winny, along with Henry Geyer, in the *Winny v. Whitesides* litigation, but also the defendants in Chouteau suits.

Joshua Barton and Edward Bates practiced law together, and when Missouri was admitted to the Union, he was the first Missouri secretary of state in 1820–21. Barton resigned from secretary of state to accept the appointment of United States district attorney for Missouri, which he held until he was killed in a duel with Thomas C. Rector on Bloody Island on June 28, 1823.[14] David Barton went on to become one of the first United States senators elected from Missouri.

Dueling was a significant part of the practice of law in Missouri at this time. Joshua Barton fought his first duel in 1816 with Thomas Hempstead. As a good law partner, Bates was Barton's second, and Thomas Hart Benton was Hempstead's second. Neither man hit his target, but apparently after both parties missed, their honor was satisfied and everyone went home.[15]

The next year, in 1817, Barton was the second to Charles Lucas in Lucas's duel with Thomas Hart Benton. Benton was a notorious duelist. Lucas was killed. Henry Geyer was Benton's second.[16]

In 1823, David Barton opposed the appointment of William Rector as surveyor general for Missouri, Illinois, and Arkansas, accusing Rector of nepotism in hiring and overpaying his relatives as surveyors in the Louisiana Purchase survey. Joshua wrote a "letter to the editor" of the *St. Louis Republican,* using the alias "Philo." Thomas Rector, William's brother, found out that Joshua had written the letter and challenged him to a duel. At 6:00 p.m. on June 30, 1823, on Bloody Island, the duel took place, and Joshua Barton was killed instantly. Thomas Rector was unhurt. Barton was taken to St. Charles for burial. Newspaper accounts referred to the duel as "a meeting" regarding the "communication signed 'Philo.'" Perhaps in part because of Barton's opposition to the appointment or perhaps because of the result of the duel, President James Monroe did not reappoint William Rector.[17] Thomas Rector was killed in 1825 in a knife fight in St. Louis. As appeared to be a lawyer custom, the local bar voted to wear "crape" on their left arms for thirty days in memory of Barton.

On July 9, 1823, the *Missouri Republican* printed an editorial stating why the "Philo" letter had been published, and stated that Rector had sent a letter to the paper stating that he "would hold the Editors responsible for any communications relating to his official conduct that might be published without the signature of the author." The editorial went on to explain that the editors felt it was the duty of a newspaper to report on and discuss the conduct of public officials regardless of threats.[18] By this time, the *Republican* was owned by Edward Charless, Joseph Charless's oldest son. Joseph was the founder of the paper.

While Joshua is more significant to us today in his involvement in the freedom suits, his brother David may also have been a plaintiff's lawyer. In *William Tarlton v. Jacob Horine,* a "D. Barton" was the plaintiff's lawyer. The "D" was never extended, but there does not seem to be another D. Barton practicing law in St. Louis at the time.

As was the custom, or perhaps fearing the worst, Joshua made out his will just prior to the duel with Rector. In Joshua's will, which was probated by Edward Bates, Barton's "esteemed and longtime friend," Barton left what he had to educate his nephew, Isaac Barton McFarlane, who was the son of his sister Hannah. If McFarlane was dead, then everything was to go to his brother David. David died in 1837. At the time of Joshua's death, Isaac was about seven years old and still living with his parents in Tennessee. Barton owned some "land in the prairie" and left it to Robert Mash, Esq. Whether this "land in the prairie" was the same 640 acres Barton owned in Jefferson County is not known. Barton's house was to go to Edward Bates as his residence for six years, then the house was to be rented to raise money for his nephew's education.[19]

Frequently, lawyers in the community would help each other out financially. On May 16, 1922, for instance, Matthias McGirk lent Barton $400, to be repaid within six months. Barton never repaid the loan, and McGirk's claim in the probate court was allowed. Four hundred dollars in 1822 would be about $7,550 today, not a huge amount, but reflective of how times could be tough even for lawyers back then.

As good a lawyer as was Joshua Barton, Peter Lindell filed a malpractice suit against Barton's estate and on July 3, 1827, got a $210.43 judgment against the estate, or about $4,000 today. Available records do not indicate the specifics of what Barton did not do or did wrong.

Peter Lindell, along with his three brothers, opened a family general store with an extensive inventory of goods. After the brothers retired from that business, they got involved in real estate and made an even larger fortune. They accumulated forty blocks in downtown St. Louis and another twelve hundred acres outside the city limits. They also ran the Lindell Hotel. Lindell Boulevard, which ran down the middle of his property, is named for Peter. A lifelong bachelor, Lindell was worth an estimated $6 million at the time of his death.

Barton Street is named after David Barton, Joshua's brother.

Edward Bates

THE QUESTION THAT WILL ALWAYS BE UNANSWERED, BUT FREQUENTLY asked, is what would have been the outcome for this nation if Edward Bates had won the Republican nomination for president in 1860. Would the South have seceded from the Union? Would slavery have survived beyond Bates's two terms as president? Given his position on slavery, preserving the Union, the development of the western territories, and the role of the government, what might this country look like today if Bates had been the first president from Missouri instead of Harry Truman?

Bates was born in Virginia in 1793 to Thomas Fleming Bates and Caroline Woodson Bates. Although his family were Quakers, his father fought in the American Revolution, which got him expelled from the Society of Friends. When Thomas finished serving in the Continental Army, his flintlock musket got handed down to the next generation of Bates men. Edward was the seventh of twelve children and came to Missouri in 1814. He came at the invitation of his brother Frederick, who was the territorial secretary at the time. Frederick was appointed to that position by President Thomas Jefferson to replace Joseph Browne, Aaron Burr's brother-in-law. Given Browne's family relationship to Burr, Jefferson felt he needed someone more loyal to himself and the nation. Frederick compiled and published the first set of territorial laws, and for a while served as acting governor. Edward's arrival was delayed because of the British invasion of Virginia during the war of 1812. Thomas Bates died in 1804, and Edward Bates got his father's old musket and went off to defend the Republic. Once that threat was resolved, Edward came to Missouri in 1814. By the time Edward arrived, Frederick had financially and socially established himself.[20]

Bates was a Whig, for as long as that party existed. The Whigs had a relatively short life, as political parties go. Founded in 1833, as the remains of the National Republican Party, the Anti-Masonic Party, and the remains of the Federalist Party, it dissolved in 1856, and what was left of its membership drifted into the Republican Party and the Know-Nothing Party. Formed in opposition to Jacksonian Democrats, Whigs favored power in the Congress over the president. The name "whigs" was a throw back to the American Whigs of 1776, who opposed British

Edward Bates, courtesy Library of Congress

tyranny. Basically supportive of what we would today call the free market system, the Whigs drew much of their support from the professional and business classes. The party split and died over the issue of the expansion of slavery into the territories. Bates never "officially" resigned from the Whig Party, but with its demise, he, along with Abraham Lincoln, found a new home in the Republican Party.

There were three things that drove Bates once he settled in Missouri: his unabiding love and devotion to his soon-to-be wife, Julia, and their family; his belief that the federal government needed to develop the western lands for better use and expansion of the territory; and his belief that the issue of slavery should not be allowed to distract from the expansion and development of Missouri and the West. The opposition to government assistance in developing western lands was led by business interests who felt that federal land should be made as cheap as possible to be sold to major financial interests. Think of this debate in terms of today's politics. Republicans believe in the "free market" system, that government should stay out of the way and let private business control the development of the country, compared to the Democrats' belief in the ability of the government to shape the nation's future for the betterment of all citizens.

While Bates owned slaves as a result of bringing his mother and sister to Missouri, he disposed of them relatively quickly, apparently as soon as they were no longer needed to care for his mother.[21] From that point on, and in reality, much earlier than that, he was opposed to slavery but felt that the issue should not be allowed to tear the country apart to the extent that the development of the West was negatively affected. Bates seemed to feel that the best solution to end slavery was to leave it where it was and keep it from spreading. Nevertheless, his personal legal practice did much to contain and eradicate slavery—certainly in the St. Louis area, where slavery was growing in more and more disfavor.

Edward studied law in the offices of Rufus Easton and was admitted to the bar in 1816. Once Edward got settled, he became one of the best-known lawyers as well as one of the most politically connected.

In 1818, with the passing of his father, Edward returned to Virginia to sort out his father's affairs and bring what was left of his family back to Missouri. The process took longer than he had hoped, but eventually, he sold off the family property, including most of the slaves, and returned to St. Louis with his mother, one sister, and about twenty slaves. The trip back to St. Louis was long because he had to come back by way of Pittsburgh to settle the estate of his brother, Tarleton, who had been killed in a duel.[22] By 1850, he had freed the remaining family slaves.

Bates was one of the delegates to the Constitution or Convention of 1822 for the admission of Missouri to the Union. He was part of what was called the "St. Louis Lawyer Group," which included the Barton Brothers, Rufus Easton, Thomas Hart Benton, John Scott, and Alexander McNair. This group of St. Louis lawyers exercised considerable influence, if not control, over the formation of the structure of Missouri government both before and after admission to the Union. In September 1820, at the first session of the Missouri General Assembly, Bates became Missouri's first attorney general. From this time on, the relationship between Bates and fellow attorney Thomas Hart Benton deteriorated. Part of the problem was their differing opinion on "hard money," and part of it was Bates's growing suspicion that Benton's real intentions were to profit himself, and that his public positions were more to ingratiate himself with the voters rather than to propound a principled position. Benton was the leader of Jacksonian Democracy in Missouri. Bates referred to Benton as "Old Bunion" because of his position on hard money and cheap land.

On May 29, 1823, Bates married Julia Coalter of South Carolina. Her father had moved his family to Missouri when Julia was a child. Edward and Julia were married in St. Charles, Missouri, and of their seventeen children, eight survived until 1860. Julia was the sister of Caroline Coulter, who married Hamilton Gamble, another ardent Whig, so the family reunion dinners were probably filled with friendly political commentary. Another of Julia's sisters married the governor of South Carolina, while a third sister married the chancellor of the University of Missouri. The Coalter sisters "married well" as went the old saying.[23]

Edward and Julia settled on the estate "Grape Hill" in St. Charles County, a day's ride from St. Louis City, which Bates farmed until his death. The family members, no matter how scattered they might be, would always return to Grape Hill for New Year's Day.

Physically, Bates was described by reporters as "a small, white-haired man, not noticeable in appearance, with a good head, sharp features, and pleasant face well-fringed with gray whiskers." He was about five feet seven inches tall, had piercing black eyes, and wore the same style Quaker clothes that he brought with him from Virginia. His black hair contrasted with his white beard.

Bates practiced law in St. Louis with Joshua Barton, who became infamous for fighting duels on Bloody Island on the Mississippi River. Being a law partner sometimes meant more than practicing law together. In 1816 Bates was the second to Barton in a duel with Thomas Hempstead, brother of Edward Hempstead, the Missouri Territory's first congressional representative. The fight ended without bloodshed. Barton would be killed later in a duel on the island in 1823. Barton's death was devastating to Bates.

Bates's career in public office was long and diverse. He was the Missouri attorney general from 1820 to 1821. Edward Bates was a member of the first Missouri Legislature and was appointed the United States attorney for the Missouri district by President James Monroe in 1824. Then Bates was a member of the U.S. House of Representatives of Missouri's at-large congressional district from March 4, 1827, through March 3, 1829, as a Whig. He was defeated for a second term. In the closing days of his term, he got into a quarrel with George McDuffie of South Carolina, who ridiculed Bates publicly on the house floor. Like any good Missouri lawyer of his day, Bates challenged McDuffie to a duel, but for good or ill, McDuffie declined the duel and publicly apologized.

Bates's dedication to the development of the West showed up in his involvement in the "River and Harbor Convention," first called in the 1840s to protest President James K. Polk's veto of the Whig-sponsored internal improvements bill, which was to improve the infrastructure of the western territories. Today we would call this a stimulus bill, or a new highway bill, but back in the 1840s, it was a fight for the federal government's involvement and funding of the public works in the West, particularly the inland waterways, the public highways of the time. The 1860 convention took place in Chicago, and 16,000 people showed up. Bates was elected president of the convention. So widespread was the involvement in the convention, that even the new, young congressman from Illinois, Abraham Lincoln, came and spoke. It was the first time that Bates and Lincoln met, and it left a positive and lasting impression on Bates. The River and Harbor Convention was a national event and represented a real debate over the future of the Louisiana Territory. Supporters of the Western Movement wanted the federal government to take the lead in developing the territory, and included such national leaders as Horace Greeley of the *New York Tribune*. Those opposing the government's involvement included many whose financial interests were in fur trading, and the private exploitation of Louisiana Territory's natural resources.

Bates was becoming more involved politically, and he became more involved in freeing slaves. During this time he became interested in the case of the slave Polly Berry, who gained her freedom decades after having been kidnapped and enslaved. Polly Berry was born around 1818 and died sometime between 1870 and 1880. Bates won the suit for her freedom in 1843 based on having been held in the free state of Illinois for a time. In 1842 Polly also sued for her daughter Lucy Ann Berry's freedom based on *partus*, which she won in 1844. What is known about Polly comes from her daughter's memoir, *From the Darkness Cometh the Light, or, Struggles for Freedom*. The book was published in 1891 under her married name, Lucy Delaney.

Bates became a prominent member of the Whig Party during the 1840s. In 1850 President Millard Fillmore asked Bates to serve as U.S. secretary of war, but he declined. Charles Magill Conrad accepted the position. At the Whig National Convention in 1852, Bates was considered for the vice-presidential slot on the ticket, and he led on the first ballot before losing on the second ballot to William Alexander Graham. Bates, a Whig, wrote one of the most vitriolic pamphlets attacking Thomas Hart Benton, a Jeffersonian Democrat, somewhat akin to the modern Republican Party. Bates fought against everything that Benton and the Democrats proposed, such things as the Homestead Act and the Oregon Treaty.

In 1853, Bates was elected to the land court and held the position until 1856 when he virtually dedicated himself to the national progress of the then Republican Party.

While the Supreme Court was deliberating the Dred Scott case, President James Buchanan was also urging the court to strike down the Missouri Compromise. Bates concluded that President Buchanan, by asserting that the Missouri Compromise unconstitutionally prohibited slavery in the territories, had reversed his narrow Jacksonian concept of the Supreme Court's role and had exercised a corruptive influence on the justices to win a decision for the stakeholders in his party and to preserve his own political position. The greatest danger to the Union, Bates declared, was that "corrupt and dangerous party"—the Democratic Party—because of its "insistence on keeping the slavery issue in public view."

Bates opposed making slavery a national issue. He thought that the issue should be resolved by allowing slavery to exist where it was then legal, and to prohibit it where it was illegal. He felt the division being caused by the national debate detracted from the more important development of the West. He was wrong in this issue, and the nation had to decide the slavery issue in order to survive. However, on the issue of slavery, Bates was unequivocal. He was opposed to it.

After the breakup of the Whig Party in the 1850s, Bates became affiliated with the Republicans and was one of four main candidates for the party's 1860 presidential nomination, receiving support from Greeley of the *New York Tribune*, who later switched to support Abraham Lincoln. Bates competed with Lincoln for the 1860 Republican nomination. Bates never became what we would call a "card carrying" Republican,

Lincoln met with his cabinet for the first reading of the "Emancipation Proclamation" draft on July 22, 1862. L-R: Edwin M. Stanton, Salmon P. Chase, Abraham Lincoln, Gideon Welles, Caleb B. Smith, William H. Seward, Montgomery Blair, and Edward Bates. Bates was the first to support Lincoln on the Emancipation; however, like a number of other leaders who supported the Emancipation, he did not support allowing freed slaves to remain in America. He supported the return of freed slaves to Africa, believing that the races, both free and equal, could not survive together. Courtesy Library of Congress

but his political "affiliations" were Republican. The Republicans mirrored his political and social philosophy more than other existing parties at the time.

The Northern Democratic Party nominated Stephen Douglas of Illinois and of the famous Lincoln-Douglas debates. The Southern Democratic Party nominated John Breckenridge of Kentucky who was vice president under James Buchanan. The Constitutional Union Party nominated John Bell of Tennessee. Bell had started out as a Democrat but fell out with Andrew Jackson and became a Whig. He was a wealthy slaveholder. The Constitutional Union Party was made up of the remnants of the Whigs and Know Nothings who were unwilling or intellectually unable to join the Democrats or the Republicans.

The 1860 Republican Convention in Chicago to select the candidate for president was perhaps as full of intrigue and campaign expertise as any until President John F. Kennedy's nomination in 1960. Doris Kearns Goodwin, in her book *Team of Rivals*, describes the people involved, the tactics, and how the convention went from a presumptive William Seward nomination to a brilliantly orchestrated Lincoln nomination.

The next year, after winning the election, Lincoln appointed Bates as his attorney general, an office Bates held from 1861 until 1864. Bates was the first cabinet member to hail from the region west of the Mississippi River. Again, Goodwin's *Team of Rivals* is an excellent resource, this time for the relationship between Bates and Lincoln.

The Civil War not only divided the nation, but also the Bates family. Although Edward Bates was for saving the Union, one of his sons, Fleming, served with the Confederates. Another son, John, served in the Union Army, and his youngest son, Charles, spent most of the Civil War at West Point.

Paying for the war was a natural topic, and Bates was keenly aware of the various means. He noted in his diary that among the plans was to initiate a 100 percent export tax on cotton, and a $10,000 "contribution" by the wealthiest 200,000 citizens. There was an additional caveat to this plan. If enough "voluntary" contributions were not made by the rich, for each $10,000 contribution, the wealthy would be given the opportunity to "draw" 5,000 acres from public lands, or about two dollars an acre. One hundred and forty years later, our Congress is debating whether during a time when the country is waging war, a reduction of the tax rate on the wealthiest 1 percent of our population is something to be enacted. How things have changed.

Another son, Barton, staying in Missouri, wrote extensively to his father during the time Bates was attorney general, and was concerned for his health. As early or late as May 13, 1864, he was trying to convince his father to resign as attorney general and come back to Missouri. Barton noted that he was quite aware that his father had not accumulated much wealth, and if he would come back, he could stay with Barton. The letter, housed in the Missouri Historical Society collection, is a touching expressions of concern of a child for his father.[24]

Bates never gave up his efforts to free slaves, and even while attorney general under Lincoln, he used his office to convince the country that the Roger Taney decision in the Dred Scott case was flawed. In 1862, a debate arose as to whether black soldiers were to be paid the same as white soldiers. The question involved, at least tangentially, was the issue of citizenship. As attorney general, in response to a request for an opinion from then Secretary of Treasury Samuel P. Chase, Bates wrote an eloquent defense of what constituted a citizen, and the first legal argument for equal pay for equal work. Bates castigated Taney's decision in the Scott case and made an eloquent argument as to the fallacy of the decision. The movie *Glory* portrayed a scene where the "colored" troops were given half the wages of the "white" soldiers.[25] This actually happened. It needs to be remembered that Judge Taney denied Dred Scott's freedom on the basis that a slave was not a person, and therefore could not be a citizen entitled to sue in the federal courts.

When Judge Taney died, Bates made an attempt to get Lincoln's appointment to the Supreme Court, which he thought would be a fitting climax to his career. He even suggested to Lincoln that he would serve only one or two years, which would give Lincoln another appointment to the Court. Lincoln appointed Samuel Chase as chief justice, and Bates took it in stride.[26]

When Lincoln was assassinated, President Andrew Johnson, influenced by Edwin Stanton, ordered a nine-man military commission to try the "conspirators." Stanton had been the attorney general under Buchanan and lost his job when Lincoln was elected. Stanton, however, retained some significant influence in Lincoln's administration by agreeing to work as a legal adviser to Simon Cameron, the secretary of war. Stanton, who later became secretary of war under Lincoln, argued for military tribunals on the basis that Lincoln was the commander-in-chief of the army, and his murder was a military crime. Bates, along with several members of the cabinet, including Gideon Welles (secretary of the navy), Orville H. Browning (secretary of the interior), and Henry McCulloch (secretary of the treasury), argued for a civil trial.[27] Unfortunately for these men, James Speed, the then attorney general, agreed with Stanton, and therefore the defendants did not enjoy the advantages of a jury trial. One hundred and fifty years later, we are still arguing over the validity of military tribunals over criminal trials in our civil courts.

Bates returned to Missouri after leaving Lincoln's cabinet. His son Barton purchased a house at Morgan and Leffingwell in St. Louis and put his father's name on the deed. In Edward's will, he acknowledged that Barton had paid for the house, and that the title should go back to him.[28] His health continued to decline, and ultimately he died in St. Louis on March 25, 1869. Eight months before he died, realizing his time was coming, Bates set down in his will on July 7, 1868, that he was dying, and was without means. His wit, humor, and love for his family came out as strong eight months before he died, as it had all his life.

In his diary, less than three years before his death and on the approach of his forty-third wedding anniversary, having acknowledged how sick he was, he wrote of his beloved Julia,

May 29, Tuesday. This is the 43d. anniversary of my marriage, and now, in old age, natural decay and sickness, our mutual love burns as brightly as in the days of our youth. God has dealt most kindly with us—He has blessed us with a large family of children, several of whom are the comfort and honor of our declining life, and he has made the course of our wedded life one unbroken stream of mutual love and enjoyment; for I declare that in the long course of 43 years, there has never been a momentary alienation or the slightest angry passage between us. Today my wife is far dearer to my heart than on the 29th of May 1823, and, in person she is still as lovely to my eye and my touch as when first delivered to my arms, in youthful beauty of sixteen.

GUSTAVUS A. BIRD

WHILE NOT ONE OF THE BEST KNOWN OR REMEMBERED LAWYERS OF HIS time, Gustavus A. Bird did leave us with a lot of information about what it was like to be a lawyer in the early 1800s. Bird was born in June 1789 in Vergennes, Vermont, graduated from Middlebury College, died in July 1846, and was buried in Christ Church Cemetery. It seems like every lawyer in the territory and state was involved in politics and the creation of the state. Bird was one of the lawyers who opposed the reappointment of Luke Lawless to circuit judge in 1837 along with Henry S. Geyer, Hamilton R. Gamble, Beverly Allen, John F. Darby, James L. English, Harris L. Sproat, Charles F. Lowry, Wilson Primm, Charles D. Drake, Ferdinand W. Risque, Alexander Hamilton, William F. Chase, Thomas B. Hudson, John Bent, and Singleton W. Wilson. We'll get into more about Lawless later, but it is important to notice the names of the lawyers who lined up on both sides of Luke Lawless being on the bench.

When Bird died, he left a widow, Hanna, and three children—John C. Bird, Amelia Bird, and Ann S. Bird.[29]

The original administrator of Bird's estate was Jennifer G. Sprigg, but for some reason, DuBouffay Fremont, the St. Louis County public administrator, seems to have taken over. Fremont was involved in selling off eighty acres of land—"Cul de Sac Common Fields"—belonging to Bird in St. Louis County and filed the final settlement.

The condition of Bird's estate appeared to be a mixed bag. He owned some property around the area and had a number of clients who apparently owed him money. There were two particularly interesting things found in Bird's probate estate. The first was that he got sued a lot. For instance:

- Judgment against Bird in suit by Anton Heeb for the use of John Sua, for breach of covenant. Heeb got a judgment against Bird in an amount of $160.40 on May 13, 1844.

- Default judgment against Bird in favor of John Wolff and John

Hoppe in the amount of $71.84 for nonpayment of a note on March 25, 1845. (I had mentioned that it seems like most lawyers at the time ran into financial straits and had to borrow money.)

- Matilda Griffeth, as the administrator for the Ada Griffeth estate, sued Bird on his bond in the probate of Ada's estate for fifty-five dollars for the failure to take care of a slave belonging to the Griffeth estate. While we have not found the original records of this suit, its description sounds incredibly interesting. Bird had posted a bond to take care of Ada's slave during the pendency of the probate. I have not found out exactly why Bird was caring for the slave, but apparently he didn't do a very good job.

While Sprigg was the administrator of the estate, she filed a petition to sell real estate because the assets of the estate were not sufficient to pay all the debts. Bird's property included "several hundred acres in St. Charles County," at least some of which Bird had agreed to rent to the board of trustees of St. Charles.

It took a long time for the ethical rule to be promulgated, requiring lawyers to get a written agreement for fees and services from their clients. Bird showed that this practice was prevalent back in the first half of the nineteenth century. Among the list of agreements entered into by Bird with clients in the probate court estate's inventory was a copy of a contingent fee contract between Bird and Henrietta Clermont where she gave Bird half interest in any recovery he could get for her in St. Louis County and a list of several fee agreements between Bird and his clients regarding his fee for representing the clients.

JOSEPH CHARLESS

THE CHARLESS FAMILY SAGA OFFERS STORIES THAT SEEM FICTIONAL, AND their tales show many facets of life in nineteenth-century St. Louis, especially the lives of Joseph Charless and his son Joseph Charless Jr.

A lawyer, newspaper publisher, and businessman, Joseph Charless Sr. took on the social and political elite. Born Protestant in Ireland, and involved in the Irish Revolution, Charless migrated to Lewiston, Pennsylvania, where he learned the printer's trade, then to Kentucky, where he was encouraged to come to St. Louis by a group of St. Louis businessmen to start the *Missouri Gazette*. A printer by trade, he was also licensed to practice law, and at the time of his death he was the president of Charless, Blow and Co., in the drug business. Charless accumulated his wealth, as most lawyers did until recent years, not from the practice of law but from his other business investments. He was a member of the Board of Aldermen for the city of St. Louis, the director of public schools, one of the directors of the Pacific Railroad, and president of the Bank of Missouri and the Mechanics Bank of St. Louis.[30]

The *Gazette*, which published its first issue on July 12, 1808, was the first newspaper printed west of the Mississippi River. The early editions were printed in English and French, in three columns, and on eight-by-twelve papers because Charless couldn't find any bigger newprint paper in St. Louis. Originally named the *Missouri Gazette*, Charles changed the name to the *Louisiana Gazette*, only to revert back to the *Missouri Gazette*.

In his newspaper activities, Charless took on the French family elite, calling the Chouteaus, John Scott, Thomas Hart Benton, and their supporters "Little Junto." His opposition to the likes of Benton continued for years. From 1808 to 1823, St. Louis was governed by a Board of Trustees, who were elected each year. With Charless publishing the *Gazette*, and Benton publishing the *Enquirer*, it was inevitable that they would run against each other and use their papers in support of their campaigns, and at different times, both won. The one time when they ran against each other, both failed to get enough votes to get elected, but

Reprint of the Missouri Gazette, *26 July 1808*

Charless gleefully printed the results, showing that although he did not get elected, he got more votes than Benton.[31]

The *Gazette* published all kinds of information about the operation of the state and city governments. For instance, in 1815, it published the financial report for St. Louis County. Charless, through his paper, campaigned for various civic improvements as well. For instance, in 1810, when the Board of Trustees authorized two fire brigades, the trustees proposed raising money by a lottery to buy the fire equipment. The lottery tickets didn't sell, and Charless proposed establishing a tax on wealthy St. Louisans to fund the fire equipment. To drive home his point, Charless ran a story about fires in Maysville, Kentucky, which destroyed a large brewery and a school.

During the War of 1812, Charless and his newspaper reflected the American bias against Indians. In 1814, two white men were killed by the Osage Indians, and Charless dutifully reported this, although the Osage were supposedly friendly to the Americans. Charless editorialized that the Osage could no longer be trusted. In order to protect the fur trade with the Indians, Pierre Chouteau, the Indian agent at the time, brought the two murderers to St. Louis for trial accompanied by several of the Osage lawyers and chiefs.

Charless had many adversaries because of his paper's abolitionist stance. Thomas Hart Benton responded by publishing the *Western Journal*, a proslavery newspaper. His outspoken editorial policy, in 1814, resulted in him being fined for contempt of court for publishing an article criticizing the court for failure to convict some Indians for killing Elijah Eastwood.

In 1820, Charless sold the paper to James Cummins, who then re-sold it to Edward Charless, Joseph's eldest son, who changed the name of the paper to the *Missouri Republican*. The paper became a six-day-a-week publication in 1836, and in 1848, the first Sunday edition appeared, raising some considerable ire from Sabbath observers. The Great Fire of 1849 destroyed a part of the *Republican*'s plant, but within two years, the plant was rebuilt, and the paper was able to use 31½ × 52-inch paper. The paper was known as the *Republic* in 1888, a name it held until it was taken over by the *St. Louis Globe-Democrat* in 1919.

Joseph Charless's involvement in the freedom suits spanned a three-year period, from 1826 to 1829. He mostly represented plaintiffs, and on the few occasions where he was co-counsel, he associated himself with the likes of Isaac McGirk and Luke Lawless. Charless died in St. Louis on July 28, 1834.

His son Joseph Charless Jr. died twenty-five years later. He was assassinated on June 4, 1859, by Joseph Thornton, who was formerly a bookkeeper at the Boatman's Savings Association. Charless had testified against Thornton when Thornton had been charged with embezzlement from the bank in 1855, when the bank had been robbed of between $18,000 and $19,000. After Thornton was dismissed from Boatman's, he began making deposits at the State Bank of Missouri in amounts from $122 to $340, totaling about $19,000. Thornton presented the bills, which were dirty and rumpled, and in one instance were so stuck together they could not be separated. The money appeared to have been buried for some time. Thornton claimed that he had gotten the money from a boatman who found it under the stump of a tree. Charless, who was president of the bank, declined to accept the deposits, claiming that the found money should be advertised so that the owner could recover the funds.

Although Thornton was acquitted, he took his revenge against Charless by assassinating him. On June 4, 1859, the day of the murder, Charless had left his home at Fifth and Walnut streets and was proceeding down Market Street toward his store. Thornton confronted Charless and said, "You are the son of a bitch that swore against my character." Thornton took out his pistol and shot Charless twice. The coroner's inquest showed that the two shots had inflicted seven separate wounds. Thornton was quickly arrested and taken to jail for his own safety, which was at what is now Fourth and Chestnut streets. A lynch mob gathered "to do violence to the unhappy prisoner," and the state militia had to be called to protect Thornton. Charless died at 7:00 a.m. the following morning at the age of fifty-five.[32] His funeral was described as the largest since the funeral of Thomas Hart Benton.[33]

Justice was swift in Missouri in the 1800s. Thornton was "expiated" on November 11, 1859, some five months after Charless's murder. The *Missouri Republican* and the *New York Times* both reported that Thornton was hung at 3:15 p.m. on November 11, 1859.[34] The newspaper description was quite vivid and described the scene.

his neck.   During this time the priests were engaged
in silent prayer.   At 3 o'clock and fourteen minutes,
the spring was touched, the door fell heavily against
the posts supporting the scaffold, and THORNTON de-
scended five feet with a sudden plunge, which broke
his neck.   For nearly three minutes his body under-
went   convulsions   and   contortions   horrible to
look upon, in which one of his hands clutched the
platform, by which he seemed to raise himself up a
moment and then drop.   Every muscle in his body
quivered with tremor, and occasionally the limbs
would writhe as though stirred with the most tumult-
uous agitation.   These spasms recurred at intervals
of thirty or forty seconds, became less and less severe,
until twenty minutes after three, when they ceased
altogether.   After the lapse of fifteen minutes, he was
taken down and placed in a metallic coffin which had

His death did not leave his family destitute or in need. William
Blow was the administrator of the probate estate. The probate bond
in the amount of $100,000 was posted by Taylor and William Blow as
principals, and John Brownlee, George Stansbury, and Henry Blow as
securities, which would indicate that Charless left an estate of about
$32 million in today's dollars. Charlotte Charless was his widow, and
Elizabeth LeBourgeois, wife of Louis LeBourgeois, was his daughter.

Probate records indicate that Charless left a substantial estate of
$25,625.88 in cash and notes, including:

- Ten shares of Bank of Missouri, twenty-five shares of Exchange
  Bank of St. Louis, thirty-five shares of Union Insurance
  Company, Pacific RR, Missouri Wine Co., Ohio and Miss RR.
  One hundred shares in the Mechanics Bank (valued at $100.00
  per share). Total value: $61,073.70

- St. Louis Agricultural & Mechanics Assoc.

- The estate listed pew no. 62 at Second Presbyterian Church at
  Fifth and Walnut, and pew no. 53 at Pine Street Presbyterian
  Church.

- Inexplicably in light of Charless's long-standing opposition to slavery, the probate court file indicates that he owned slaves worth $1,000, and his interest in Charless, Blow & Co. was worth $299,820.63 in 1859 dollars, or about $8 million in today's dollars.

- Inventory indicates he owned real estate in four pieces in Iowa, one in Illinois, fifteen pieces in Missouri outside St. Louis, eight outside the city of St. Louis, eleven pieces in Carondelet, and three in the city of St. Louis.

His widow, Charlotte, applied for one year's support in the amount of eighteen hundred dollars on September 23, 1859. The probate file also indicates that Charless had pledged one thousand dollars to Westminster College for scholarships in ten installments at 6 percent interest on July 16, 1855. There does not seem to be any other connection between Charless and Westminster College.

The Charless Home, a retirement home in the Southern portion of St. Louis City, was founded by Joseph Charless Jr.'s wife, Charlotte Taylor Blow Charless a "Home of the Friendless" in St. Louis in 1853 for elderly, indigent women who could no longer work and care for themselves. It was renamed "The Charless Home" in 1977, the institution celebrated its 150th anniversary in 2003 and continues to provide housing and services to retired men (since 1996) as well as women.

Horatio Cozens

Horatio Cozens teamed up with George Strother in a law practice in the early 1820s when Strother was representing the defendants. Now and then, in every profession, there are lives that tradition sets apart and crowns with peculiar sacredness, seemingly without definite reason except that they were brief, brilliant, and tragic. Such a life was that of Horatio Cozens.

Cozens was born on January 13, 1795, in Philadelphia to William Cozens and Charlotte Nicholas and moved to Missouri from Virginia shortly before Missouri became a state. He married Anne Caroline Sanguinet, the daughter of Charles Sanguinet and Marie Anne Conde, on November 24, 1818, in St. Louis King of France (the Old Cathedral) when Anne was eighteen years old. She died on New Year's Day in 1884. They had four children: Marie Cozens, born 1819; Charlotte Cozens, born about 1819; William H. Cozens, born 1820; and James Cozens, born 1820.

With a reputation as an eloquent speaker and a trial lawyer, when Cozens was twenty-six or twenty-seven, he had a complete falling out with George F. Strother, whom he described as a dissipated and unprincipled man.

Strother had a nephew named French Strother, another young lawyer, who undertook to vindicate his uncle George. The problem apparently arose when Cozens was trying a lawsuit before a Judge Penrose. French Strother entered the courtroom and indicated to Cozens that someone wanted to speak with him outside the courtroom. Cozens went outside with French, who then stabbed Cozens in the heart. Cozens died within minutes.

Strother was immediately arrested, and it was all that the local law-enforcement officials could do to save him from being lynched by a mob. Strother was described as twenty-four years old, five feet six inches tall, with brown hair, a light complexion, blue eyes, and somewhat near-sighted with a "taciturn disposition."

Strother, however, broke out of jail and fled to Mexico, where he led a dissipated life and finally died. The escape was described in the *Missouri Republican* as having taken place on September 27, 1826, as a breakout along with Patrick Saye, a convicted murderer, and John Brewer, who had been sentenced to be executed. The three had dug through a four-foot-thick stone wall. A five hundred-dollar reward was posted for their capture.

Newspaper accounts of the day report that members of the St. Louis Bar met on July 15, 1826, to adopt a resolution that all of them would wear crape on their left arm in honor of Cozens.

When he died, Cozens left no will. His estate was administered by his widow Anne Caroline Cozens, Louis Benoist, and Joseph V. Garnier. Benoist was a wealthy real estate investor who moved to St. Louis from New Orleans. The estate's attorney was a lawyer named John Darby, who put up a $4,000 bond in probate court, which would indicate an estimated personal property value of $76,000.[35]

Among the claims against the estate were:

- *State of Missouri v. Horatio Cozens* for malpractice with judgment in favor of the state in an amount of $176 entered on October 19, 1824.

- *John Walker v. Horatio Cozens* for malpractice with judgment in the amount of $99.27 on March 28, 1826.

- James Benson filed a malpractice suit and got a judgment for $140.66 on August 2, 1825.

- Default judgment in favor of William Grindsley on a promissory note for $32.44 entered on April 10, 1826. The estate asked to have the judgment set aside, denied, and appealed. The appeal bond was never perfected.

It looks like Cozens borrowed a lot of money in the early 1820s: A petition to sell real estate listed debts totaling $1,773.72, and said Cozens did not have assets sufficient to pay the debts, so real estate had to be sold. Among the assets he left were:

- A mulatto named Louis sold by the estate and bought by Robert Wash by his agent William H. Ashley for $220, but Louis was sick at the time of the sale, and stayed sick after the sale. The sale was set aside on November 9, 1827. Strother's slave ownership may give some indication as to his propensity to represent other slave owners in the freedom suit. As an illustration as to how close the St. Louis community was even back in the early 1800s, Robert Wash from the Polly Berry freedom suit—which is described in detail later in the book—was the widower of Fanny Berry, who refused to free the Berry slaves in accord with Fanny's husband's will, and who sold Polly Berry's husband down the river.

Among the real estate that had to be sold to pay off the estate's debts were:

- 200 arpens in Lincoln County "in what is called the 'Kings Bay'" sold on the third Monday of June 1847;
- 1,000 arpens in Franklin County sold to John Darby for $134.00 on "the first Tuesday after the first Monday in February 1848";
- Ralls County property, may have become property in Marion County, sold on the first Monday of July 1847;
- land in Big Prairie west of St. Louis;
- lot in St. Louis;
- four sections of land in Illinois; and
- a lot in Pike County, Illinois.

It took nearly twenty-three years to settle the estate. The final settlement was filed on March 24, 1849, with what looks like $329 left over and was paid to John Darby, the attorney.

He was buried at the Roman Catholic cemetery for twenty dollars, as was reflected by the claim allowed on December 9, 1826.

Rufus Easton

Occasionally, in the history of Missouri we come across giants, people whose contributions were so large that they literally changed the history of the nation. Surprisingly, however, their story disappears from our collective memory. Rufus Easton is one of these giants. He was a preeminent lawyer, and he trained some of the very best lawyers in St. Louis.

Born in Litchfield, Connecticut, Easton studied law, was admitted to the bar, and practiced in Rome, New York. He moved to Vincennes, Indiana, in 1804, then to St. Louis, where he was appointed district judge and postmaster in 1805, a position he served until 1815. Easton built the first post office west of the Mississippi in St. Louis at Third and Elm streets where the St. Louis Arch rests today.

Easton was extremely sought after as a teacher and mentor by people wanting to study law in St. Louis. In 1815, Edward Bates moved into the Easton home, studied law, and became Easton's law partner. In addition to Bates, Easton also taught law to Charles Lucas, Joshua Barton, and Rufus Pettibone. The history of these men and their contributions to the freedom suits are outlined in their own chapters. But at the time, if you wanted to study law under the very best, you hoped to have Rufus Easton as your teacher.

Easton was involved, although tangentially, in thwarting Aaron Burr's efforts to remove the Louisiana Territory from the United States. When Burr resigned as vice president, he came to St. Louis in 1805 to explore his opportunities in the Louisiana Territory. General James Wilkinson, who was the commander of the U.S. Army and the acting governor of the Upper Louisiana, was friendly to Burr. When Burr came to St. Louis, he stayed with the general, who introduced Burr to some of the leading members of St. Louis, including Easton. Burr told Easton enough of his plans for the West to convince Easton to have nothing more to do with him. Within a few days of his October 1805 meeting with Burr, Easton wrote to President Thomas Jefferson that Wilkinson had aligned himself with Burr and some others whose interests were hostile to those of the national government. After a later meeting with the president, Easton made a full report of Burr's activities to the president. Although Burr got no encouragement from the local leaders in St. Louis, General Wilkinson remained hostile to Easton and started rumors of Easton's official misconduct. Easton ended this by going to Washington to meet with President Jefferson.[36]

Easton was among the first to advocate statehood for Missouri, and he wanted Missouri to be admitted as a free state. In 1822, however, he was co-counsel with Edward Barton and Rufus Pettibone, two of his students, representing Henry Hight, who was being sued by his slave, Susan (represented by Matthias McGirk).

Unlike a number of other frontier lawyers, Easton managed to avoid four duels, the most notable of which was one with Aaron Burr, at the urging of Lincoln's postmaster general, Gideon Granger.[37]

Starting as early as 1805, Easton was intimately involved in the legal process in St. Louis. That year, President Jefferson was appointing territorial officers and named Rufus as one of the three original judges. Easton was at odds with the then territorial governor, General Wilkinson, also appointed by Jefferson. The basis of the feud was Easton's opposition to the major Spanish land grants on the charge of fraudulent land purchases. Wilkinson, on the other hand, sided with the old French and the new American allies. Ultimately, the fight between Wilkinson and Easton was resolved when President Jefferson did not reappoint Easton to the bench.[38]

Easton's clients included some of the Iowa Indian Tribe. In 1807, a band of Iowa Indians killed some white traders. The American authorities convinced the Iowas to turn over those responsible for the attacks.

The two Indians turned over were tried and convicted, but Rufus Easton became the attorney for the tribe. On appeal, he won a retrial. The successful appeal, however, didn't change the ultimate result.[39] On the retrial, the Indians were convicted. The frontier Americans saw the Iowas as a source of constant trouble because they were on the front door of the Osage Indian Tribe. An the Osage were even more feared and disdained by settlers.

Upon the organization of the Missouri state government in 1821, Easton was appointed attorney general and served until 1826. He engaged in the practice of law and primarily in the real estate business. Easton died in St. Charles, Missouri, on July 5, 1834. He was interred in the Lindenwood College Cemetery. Lindenwood College was founded by his daughter, Mary Easton Sibley. Among his survivors were seven daughters, some of whom went on to marry the most distinguished men of the Louisiana Territory: George Sibley, commissioner of the Santa Fe Trail and business manager of the Osage Indian Nation; Archibald Gamble, ninth postmaster of St. Louis and brother of Missouri's Civil War governor, Hamilton Gamble; Henry S. Geyer, attorney before the U.S. Supreme Court in the Dred Scott case; Robert Simpson, second postmaster of St. Louis; Senator Thomas Anderson; and Abner Bartlett of New York, who was in charge of William Waldorf Astor's estate from 1869 to 1894.[40]

Easton was also one the founders of the Bank of St. Louis, which opened in 1814. The following year, the Bank of Missouri was established. Even back in this early history of St. Louis, everyone was within two degrees of relationship. The political influence of these banks and their shareholders ran until statehood. One of the greatest advantages of creating your own bank was the ability to print your own money.

Easton Avenue was changed to Dr. Martin Luther King Jr. Drive.

Roswell M. Field

The Motivation for early Americans to come to Missouri to start a new life varied greatly. Some came for the adventure, the chance to make one's fortune in furs or politics. In the case of Roswell M. Field, it was a family scandal and shame. In St. Louis, he was one of the lawyers who represented Dred and Harriet Scott, but he is perhaps best remembered as the father of the poet Eugene Field.

Field was born in Newfane, Vermont, on February 22, 1807, the third of four children. His father, Martin, was a lawyer and a general in the American Army during the Revolutionary War. Roswell enrolled at Middlebury College at the age of eleven and graduated in 1822 when he was fifteen years old. He studied law with his uncle, Daniel Kellogg, for three years and was admitted to the Vermont Bar in 1825. He practiced in Mendham County, Vermont, for fourteen years and moved to St. Louis in 1839, following his brief marriage to a woman who had been previously promised in marriage to another man.[41]

Field met Mary Ann Phelps, who at the time was engaged to Jeremiah Clark. Miss Phelps and Roswell were quickly taken with each other, although the engagement to Clark was known to Field. Mary Ann's mother suspected something was amiss and ordered her daughter home. On October 15, on the trip home, with Roswell inexplicably accompanying her, she and Roswell got married. The couple apparently agreed that they would not consummate the marriage, and if she did not want to consummate the marriage when she got home, they would consider the marriage null and void. When Mary Ann got home to Windsor, she neglected to mention her marriage to Field to anyone. On October 29 she wrote to Clark, who lived in Boston, and asked him to come to Windsor. When Clark arrived, Mary Ann told him and her family about her marriage to Field. On the same day, she wrote to Field telling him that upon further reflection she decided that their marriage was a mistake, and she never wanted to see him again.

I leave you to the alternative of forever preventing the public avowal of a disgraceful transaction, of which you yourself said you were ashamed.

On November 27, she married Clark.

Field and Mary Ann filed, quietly, in the Vermont chancery court, to have their marriage annulled on the grounds that they did not intend to consummate the marriage at the time of the wedding, and so the marriage was not valid. This theory, that the union was not valid unless the parties intended to consummate the marriage at the time of the wedding, was accepted by the court more for the purpose of preventing Mary Ann from being accused of being an adulteress and bigamist than on following any accepted principal of marital law that existed in Vermont at the time.[42] Given the social situation, and the families involved, this incredible fiasco may have been the reason Field felt he had to move west.

Interestingly, years later, when both Roswell's wife and Mary Ann's husband died, Mary Ann came to St. Louis to visit Roswell in the hope of reigniting the old fire. But Roswell declined to see her, and she returned to Vermont without a husband.

Roswell Field began his St. Louis law practice emphasizing disputed real estate title cases. When he first came to St. Louis, he took up lodging in a boarding house with a German family, where he resided for three years. His Middleberry College education meant that he could speak German, French, and Spanish. During the first six years of his practice, he survived on gifts of money from his father. Eventually, he met and married Frances Maria Reed in 1848. Their first son, Theodore, died in the Cholera Epidemic of 1849, which killed more than four thousand people in St. Louis. By the time of the birth of their second son, Eugene, in 1850, Roswell and Frances moved south of downtown on Fifth Street. Mrs. Field died in November 1856, and the following year Eugene and his younger brother, Roswell, were sent to school in Amherst, Massachusetts, and lived with their paternal aunt, Mary, and their cousin, Mary Field French. Amherst is about fifty miles from Newfane.

The Eugene Field House and St. Louis Toy Museum, the former residence of Roswell Field, at 634 S. Broadway.

Field was an outspoken abolitionist, which was what drew him to represent Dred and Harriet Scott in their suit for freedom. He came into the fray late, after the case had been appealed to the Missouri Supreme Court by the owner of the Scotts, Mrs. Emerson, in 1850. Field agreed to take the Scotts' case after two trials, which they won, and two hearings in the state supreme court, which they lost, for no fee. Field filed the suit in the federal court because Mrs. Emerson had moved to New York and the fact of having citizens of more than one state as parties to the case allowed a federal suit. The federal case was filed in St. Louis in

1853 and tried in 1854 on an agreed stipulation of facts. Judge Robert Wells ultimately decided that, although Dred Scott was a citizen and had the right to bring the suit, the taking of the Scotts into Illinois only suspended their status as slaves, and the return to Missouri reinstated their slavery.

The rest is, as they say, history, and Judge Roger Taney infamously decided that Dred and his family were not persons and did not have the right to file the suit in the first place.

Field got involved with freedom suits in 1840. During the first half of the 1840s, he and Francis Murdoch took on a few of the suits with varying degrees of success. Murdoch was much more involved in the freedom suits on his own. Bates, Geyer, and the earlier lawyers from the 1820s pretty much dropped out of the picture by this time. In 1843, Field represented Thomas Jefferson in a suit against Milton Hopkins. In 1844, he represented two slaves, James and Martha Ann, in a suit against Hiram Cordell, as well as Cloe Ann against Franklin Knox, and lastly in 1845, he represented Rachel Steele against Thomas Taylor.

Roswell, Field, and Eugene avenues, south of Carondelet Park, honor Field family members. Plus, the Eugene Field House and St. Louis Toy Museum, at 634 S. Broadway, was opened as St. Louis's first historic house museum in 1936. It was Eugene Field's childhood home, and Roswell's home during his professional prime.

THOMAS T. GANTT

THOMAS T. GANTT GENERALLY REPRESENTED PLAINTIFFS WITH GEORGE Strother and was considered a submissionist, which was the term used by Southern secessionists in the year preceding the Civil War to describe Southerners, many of them slave owners, who wanted to preserve the Union. Before 1861, Southerners loyal to the Union were generally respected as principled idealists. As Southern states began to actually secede, however, Southerners who remained Unionists were viewed as cowardly and lacking the strength to stand up for their own rights. Following the winter of 1861, popular sentiment in the Deep South held that the North was unwilling to compromise with the South. The Deep South would rather secede from the Union than relinquish sovereignty. Consequently, "submissionist" was a derogatory name for a Southerner who would seemingly relinquish sovereignty in order to remain in the Union.

The term was used also to describe a particular kind of cooperationist, that is, one who is generally opposed to secession. Louisiana politician, Pierre Soulé, for instance, a cooperationist, protested that he was "no submissionist" and would choose revolution (i.e., secession) rather than ignominy. Gantt, however, provost marshal general of the district of Missouri, proudly called himself a submissionist at the Missouri State Convention on March 15, 1861. Edmund Ruffin, who is credited with firing the first shot at the battle of Fort Sumter, noted in his diary on September 3, 1861, "As a general rule, the submissionist party embraces, & is largely composed of, the old, the timid, the cowardly, the imbecile & the mean-spirited."

Gantt was one of the early supporters of gun control in St. Louis. He was a key member of the constitutional drafting committee of 1875, which contained a ban on concealed weapons. Relying on his experience in St. Louis with the riotous Know Nothings, he declared of the history of Missouri, "this shall not justify the wearing of concealed weapons. It is a practice which cannot be too severely condemned. It is a practice fraught with the most incalculable evil."[43] Now that the Missouri Legislature has overturned the popular vote of Missourians, and rejected the view of Missouri's founding fathers, we find that the lessons of history have not been learned very well.

Henry S. Geyer

Henry S. Geyer was born in Frederick, Maryland, in December 1790. He studied privately in the offices of his maternal uncle, Daniel Shaeffee, a well-respected lawyer, and was admitted to the Maryland Bar in 1811. He fought as a lieutenant from 1813 to 1815 as a paymaster with the Maryland infantry during the War of 1812, stationed in Norfolk, Virginia. In 1815, he moved to Missouri, still as a paymaster and began to practice law on the side. Apparently, the job of paymaster was a part-time job with the military. By the end of 1815, he resigned his military commission to practice law full time. During this time, he somehow also obtained a commission as captain of the first military company organized west of the Mississippi, and was called "Captain" for the rest of his life.

He was described as a hot-tempered, sharp-tongued Irishman. He had an acerbic wit and enjoyed poking fun at others for his own amusement and at others' expense. He was considered cold, selfish, reserved, and didn't have many friends outside his immediate family. Given his temper and tongue, he got into a dueling feud with another military captain by the name of George Kennerby in 1816. No one recalls the origins or details of the feud, but it ended in a duel on Bloody Island where Geyer wounded Kennerby so severely that Kennerby was unable to continue with the second round. By the intervention of a mutual friend, the feud was settled, and Kennerby continued as one of Geyer's few friends for the rest of their lives.

Geyer became a member of the Territorial Assembly in 1818 and was a delegate to the Missouri Constitutional Convention in 1820. He served in the Missouri House of Representatives from 1820 to 1824, and again in 1834 to 1835. He authored the Geyer Act in 1839, which established public education in Missouri and the University of Missouri. Geyer was involved in the drafting of virtually every piece of major legislation.

Despite his unpleasant personality, he was considered one of the top all-around lawyers in St. Louis. His reputation as a lawyer put him

in nearly every major Spanish land grant litigation in Missouri.[44]

His most publicly celebrated case was *State v. Darnes,* tried in 1840, a case that drew tremendous attention from the social, legal, and medical communities. Darnes was indicted for manslaughter for killing a Mr. Davis, who was the publisher of the *Argus,* a Democratic newspaper. William Gilpin was the editor, and Davis, who had nothing to do with the editorial content of the paper, was a small, quiet, unassuming man who never got into fights with anyone. An article appeared in the *Argus* denouncing a certain "class" of politicians, and Darnes thought the article referred to him. Darnes demanded an explanation from Davis, who refused. The next day, Colonel Gilpin, always ready for a fight, admitted he was the author of the editorial and said he would take on anyone who was offended. This is shorthand for accepting any challenge (duel) anyone wanted. Darnes was a tall, stout man, but somewhat of a cowardly cad. Instead of accepting Gilpin's challenge, Darnes waylaid Davis near the National Hotel at Third and Market streets and beat him mercilessly with an iron cane. Davis was taken to a hotel and died eight days later. In an attempt to save Davis, Dr. William Beaumont, a skilled surgeon, performed what was known as a trephining, a dangerous surgery to relieve the pressure on the brain caused by the beating from Darnes.

Geyer's defense was that Beaumont's surgery was the cause of Davis's death, not Darnes's beating. (This was perhaps one of the first times that medical malpractice was claimed as a defense in a manslaughter charge.) The cream of the St. Louis medical community testified at the trial, and the prosecution put poor Davis's skull into evidence both to show the extent of injuries and to let the doctors explain the operation. Eventually, Darnes was convicted of third- or fourth-degree manslaughter (the record is unclear), which at the time was the equivalent of an acquittal.

Ardently proslavery, Geyer inexplicably represented both sides in the various freedom suits. Geyer's final role in the freedom suits was as attorney for the defendant slave owner against Dred Scott in the United States Supreme Court in 1856. Representing the defendant in the U.S. Supreme Court while in office as a U.S. senator evidently was not unseemly at the time. Geyer had always wanted to be a U.S. senator and was ultimately elected as a Whig and served from March 4, 1851, to March 4, 1857. He did not run for reelection and resumed the practice of law in St. Louis. His senatorial career is generally considered "disappointing" and undistinguished, which shows that sometimes a great trial lawyer makes a terrible elected official.

Geyer ultimately became a St. Louis judge, and perhaps, exhibiting his proslavery bent, notably excused the mob who burned a mulatto at the stake by placing the blame for the mob's actions on the abolitionists.

Geyer died at 10:00 p.m. at his home in St. Louis on March 5, 1859, at the age of sixty-nine. He was buried from his home and interred at Bellefontaine Cemetery. In an article that appeared in the *St. Louis Globe-Democrat*, it was commented that "veteran lawyers seldom succeed as statesmen and legislators," referring to his earlier public career that was followed by a subsequent devotion to the practice of law. While he had been ill, he was "rumored" to be recovering when he took a turn for the worse and died suddenly of a "rupture of the heart." The *Missouri Republican* listed among his achievements: member of the Constitutional Convention that framed the Missouri Constitution, member of the Missouri General Assembly, twice-elected speaker of the Missouri House of Representatives, U.S. senator, close friend of Henry Clay, and man-without-a-party as the Whigs disintegrated and disappeared. On March 7, 1859, the members of the St. Louis Bar held a meeting and service for Geyer, which again included the customary "badge of mourning for thirty days."[45]

He may have been the most prolific lawyer from St. Louis at the time to argue before the U.S. Supreme Court, with appearances in *Farrar v. United States*, 30 U.S. 373 (1831); *Strother v. Lucas*, 37 U.S. 410 (1838); *Marsh v. Brooks*, 49 U.S. 223 (1850); *Marsh v. Brooks*, 55 U.S. 513 (1852); *Delaurier v. Emison*, 56 U.S. 525 (1853); *McCabe v. Worthington*, 57 U.S. 86 (1853); *Guitard Stoddard*, 57 U.S. 494 (1853); *Kissell v. St. Louis Public Schools*, 59 U.S. 19 (1855); *Ham v. Missouri*, 59 U.S. 126 (1855); *Griffith v. Bogert*, 59 U.S. 158 (1855); *Long v. O'Fallon*, 60 U.S. 116 (1856); *Meegan v. Boyle*, 60 U.S. 130 (1856); *Garrison v. Memphis Ins. Co.*, 60 U.S. 312 (1856); *Dred Scott v. Sandford*, 60 U.S. 393 (1856); and his last appearance before his death, *Goodman v. Simonds*, 61 U.S. 343 (1857).

The Kissell case had and continues to have substantial significance to property that was originally dedicated for a specific use, such as Tower Grove Park, dedicated by Henry Shaw, and Saint Mary and Joseph Church in the Carondelet area.

The probate file for Henry S. Geyer shows that his will was executed on September 14, 1858.[46] His wife, at the time of his death, was Jane L. Geyer. He left four children: deceased son Edward, Henry, daughters Marial C., wife of James Small, and Harriet G., wife of James Norris. The executor was James F. Small, who was required to post a probate bond of $30,000, which would indicate an estate of $820,000, excluding real estate.

Geyer reinstated all of the property to Jane, which she owned at the time of their marriage, and so waived any claim he may have for dower.

Although proslavery, the only slave he owned at his death was a mulatto, William, about twenty-nine years old, who was given to his wife, for her life, and then freed. If Jane were to die before Henry, William was to go free at Henry's death.

Henry had Geyer Avenue named after him.

LUKE LAWLESS

LAWLESS WAS NEVER CONFUSED WITH SOMEONE WHO WAS IN FAVOR OF freedom suits. As a judge, he justified the killing of a black dockworker by a mob. In 1836, Francis McIntosh, a free black steamboat steward from Pittsburgh, was burned alive by a mob in downtown St. Louis after killing a deputy sheriff attempting to arrest two black fellow crew members.[47] The episode divided the city, simultaneously rallying support for control of nonwhites even as it outraged opponents of slavery and its racialized violence. While one newspaper described the episode as a regrettable but necessary warning "for impudent free Negroes to be *cautious*," Elijah Lovejoy's *St. Louis Observer* denounced the city's inaction in preventing the lynching. "[T]he question lies between justice regularly administered or the wild vengeance of a mob," a choice which left "but one side on which the patriot and Christian can rally; but one course for them to pursue."[48] Following Judge Luke Lawless's instructions that the jury must identify specific persons as responsible for seizing and setting fire to McIntosh, a St. Louis grand jury refused to indict anyone. Lovejoy's denunciation of the outcome led to mob attacks on his press, which in turn generated warnings about a descent into mob rule and the end of the rule of law.[49] Lawless generally represented slaveholders in his law practice, although for some reason he represented slave Francois LaGrange in 1827 against Pierre Chouteau and Jean Cabanne.

Another example of Lawless's proslavery attitude was the instructions he gave to the jury in *Rachel v. Walker*. Walker, an army officer, argued that he did not take his slave, Rachel, into the free state voluntarily, as he was assigned to duty there. Lawless bought the argument and instructed the jury accordingly.[50]

The number of lawyers who opposed Lawless for his rulings and judicial demeanor included Eugene Bates, and the fight with Lawless culminated in Lawless's personal attacks on Judge James Peck. Peck had ruled against Lawless's clients in a land claim case. Lawless attacked the integrity of Peck in the papers. Peck, understandably, thought little of the attacks, jailed Lawless for contempt of court, and disbarred him. Lawless had friends, including Thomas Hart Benton, who initiated impeachment proceedings against Peck. Peck was acquitted, but Benton had the last word when the Democrats consolidated their power and elevated Lawless to circuit judge. As a matter of fact, Lawless served as Benton's second when Benton was killed in a duel.[51]

Lawless was the judge in *BCL v. Bishop Joseph Rosati*. He also argued several cases in the U.S. Supreme Court, including: *Smith v. Honey*, 28 U.S. 469 (1830); *Lagrange v. Chouteau*, 29 U.S. 287 (1830); *Strother v. Lucas*, 37 U.S. 410 (1838); *Chouteau v. Eckhart*, 43 U.S. 344 (1844); and *Mackay v. Dillon*, 45 U.S. 421 (1846).

Probate court records reflect that his will was dated October 26, 1832, leaving everything to his wife, Virginia. The administrator was Alex J. Garesche, although for some reason Virginia was named the executor in the will and renounced her right to be the executor and asked that an administrator be named. Assets listed in Lawless's will included lands to which George F. Strother and he had agreed to divide amongst themselves.

ISAAC MCGIRK

WHEN ISAAC MCGIRK DIED AT 10:00 P.M. ON FEBRUARY 8, 1830, THE administrator of his will was Josiah Spalding. There was no mention of a widow or children in his will. McGirk provided that any surplus remaining in his estate after debts were paid go to his brother Matthias McGirk, and he willed that Matthias make a fund for the support, maintenance, and education of a certain female child called Brunetta, the daughter of a free colored woman named Harriet. "I desire that said child shall remain under the control and direction of the said Matthias until she shall be married or arrive at the age of twenty-one and that if before either event she shall be withdrawn from his control he shall not from that time apply the said fund or its proceeds to her use but the same shall be distributed as if I died in intestate."

If married with Matthias's consent, Isaac willed that Matthias shall pay to Brunetta the principal of that fund, but no money if she married without consent. "I make the foregoing provisions for the support of the said child in performances of what I consider a sacred duty and from the desire to make her as respectable in the world as circumstances will admit."

McGirk also stated that if Brunetta dies before the age of twenty-one or before married then the money was to be divided between Isaac Scott of east Tennessee (nephew), Isaac McGirk (son of brother Andrew McGirk), and Isaac McGirk (son of brother John McGirk). The principal asset was 160 acres of land deeded to him by John McGilman in the County of Chariton, Missouri. Final settlement was made on August 6, 1833, distributing approximately $2,376.72. There is little mention of either Harriet or Brunetta in the histories of Isaac, and so we may never know the nature of their relationship.

Rufus Pettibone

ANOTHER OF THE NOTED LAWYERS OF THIS FORMATIVE ERA IN MISSOURI was Judge Rufus Pettibone, who was born in Litchfield, Connecticut, into a large family in May 1784. Pettibone graduated from Williams College in 1805, taking high honors. Adopting the legal profession, he studied in Central New York State, and afterwards in Albany, where he was admitted to the bar in 1808. In 1812, Oneida County elected him to represent it in the legislature, and the next year he married Louise Esther De Russey. Five years later, in 1817, he decided to move to Missouri with his wife and three children, and for some reason he was offered a partnership with Rufus Easton, one of the best lawyers in St. Louis and one of the leaders of the bar.[52]

Even at this early date, many people in the territory were opposed to slavery. The question of the spread of slavery into Missouri, especially at the time of the admission of Missouri into the Union was being considered, split the bar, as it did the general population. While seemingly a minority, there were a significant number of respected lawyers who opposed slavery in Missouri. A slate of these lawyers was proposed for the initial legislature. The slate—consisting of J. B. C. Lucas, Rufus Easton, Rufus Pettibone, Robert Simpson, and Caleb Bowles—was well aware it was in a hopeless minority. They were supported by Joseph Charless and the *Missouri Gazette*. Interestingly, among these lawyers was Rufus Pettibone. Although not elected, he was appointed, along with Henry Geyer, to revise the Missouri laws in 1824 and 1825.

Pettibone's representation of defendants is all the more confusing since he apparently was a slave owner, having been sued in 1825 by a few plaintiffs, and was named in one of the Winny suits as a defendant.

In 1824, he was appointed as judge for the second judicial circuit, which consisted of Ralls, Pike, Lincoln, St. Charles, Montgomery, and Callaway counties on the north side of the Missouri River, and Gasconade County on the south side. He lived in St. Charles until 1823 when he was appointed to the supreme court; however, his term was short. In the winter of 1824 to 1825, in conjunction with Henry S. Geyer, he revised Missouri state laws and prepared them for legislative enactment. On July 31, 1825, in the fullness of his powers, he died, and the state lost one of its most valued citizens. Geyer announced his death in the St. Louis Circuit Court, and it, as well as the supreme court, adjourned with the usual marks of respect.

JOSIAH SPALDING

JOSIAH SPALDING DIED IN 1852, HAVING PREPARED HIS WILL ON MAY 18, 1849. He left everything to his wife, Agnes, should she survive him. If Agnes should die before Josiah, then one fourth of his estate was to be held in trust for his son, Edward, and the remaining three shares to be distributed among his three daughters—one to each. If any of the children should die before reaching twenty-one, and leave no children, their share was to go to the other surviving children. His daughters were Julia, who was married to William T. Reynolds, Mary, and Anna.

Spalding's executors were Alexander Hamilton and Joseph and John Shepley. However, on May 25, 1852, Hamilton and the Shepleys declined to be appointed executors and nominated Spalding's wife, Agnes, who was appointed.

The probate bond was in the amount of $60,000. The assets included:

Real estate
4th & Cedar - "the Mansion House"; Lewis & Tiffany; 28th and Didier; 2nd St. In North St. Louis; 2 lots at 2nd & Howard; 2 lots on the east side of Maine & Florida; 2nd between Howard and Payne; Howard & Broadway at 2,000 acres in Lee County, Iowa; 28 lots in Sibley, Jackson County, Missouri.

The value of his personal property was $45,234.67.

There is some indication that Spalding was a partner with Shepley and Tiffany, in a business having an additional value of $10,000.

There were a number of claims made against the estate, which included: Judgment against estate on April 25, 1854, in favor of Briffey Fremons administrator for testee of John T. Barr in amount of $545.85.

The final settlement indicated a distribution of $23,930.63

George F. Strother

George French Strother was the father of James French Strother and great-grandfather of another named James French Strother. Born in Stevensburg, Virginia, in 1783, he attended the College of William and Mary. Strother then studied law and practiced in Culpeper County, Virginia. He was a member of the Virginia House of Delegates from 1806 to 1809 and was later elected as a Democratic-Republican to the U.S. House of Representatives in 1816, serving from 1817 to 1820. He married Theodosia Hunt on May 1, 1825. George and Theodosia had what appeared to be five children, James F. Strother, John Hunt Strother, who died in 1853 in Europe, Sally Williams Strother, who died on April 22, 1885, and two additional daughters, mentioned by name in local news accounts of his death—Pink Hamilton and Mrs. Theodore Foster. Theodosia died shortly before George, who died on November 28, 1840. He was originally interred in Christ Church Cemetery and was later reinterred in Bellefontaine Cemetery in 1860. Historically, his principal claim to fame was that his nephew assassinated Horatio Cozens.

Strother was a slaveholder but was one of several abolitionist lawyers who represented slaves in the freedom suits.

In 1822, he and several other Presbyterians started raising money for a new Presbyterian church in St. Louis, on Fourth Street between St. Charles and Washington avenues.

Strother died at the age of seventy-one without a will. His longtime friend, Alexander Hamilton, was appointed administrator. The principal assets of the estate were:

- Cash account at Bank of Missouri—$29,381.14; branch at Ste. Genevieve—$45,963.38;
- Personal property (household items)—$274.27.

The real estate included property in Pike County (2,414 acres); Cole

County; Callaway County; St. Louis County; Gasconade County; and Wayne County.

He left three slaves to Theodosia named William, Mary, and Susan, but there is an affidavit in the probate file from his son James stating that his father sold three Negroes (William, Mary, and Susan) for the sum of fifteen hundred dollars in 1833. The gift was useless since Theodosia died prior to Strother.

The claims against his estate included:

- A suit by Francis A. Dickins in Washington, D.C. Dickens was hired by Strother to get a bill passed in Congress, Dickins claimed he was never paid by Strother and therefore was suing the estate. There is no mention in the file as to which bill. However, it looks like the estate ended up paying Dickins an amount not indicated in the probate records.

- There were approximately fifty IOUs from clients to Strother in the file dating from the years 1820 to 1842.

The amount of said estates on March 21, 1846, was $652.01. It looks like Hamilton then itemized his fees for $282.76, leaving $369.25 to estate.

Hamilton filed a petition to the court for additional time to file inventory on June 8, 1841, stating that he was having difficulties figuring out the estate due to the "chaotic state" of Strother's papers. On March 20, 1846, Hamilton filed a pleading to the court stating "the estate of said deceased is largely indebted." The annual settlement was filed on June 16, 1846, showing a balance of $662.99.

THE JUDGES

THE THREE JUDGES WHO CLEARLY ESTABLISHED THE RIGHT OF SLAVES TO GET their freedom were Matthias McGirk, George Tompkins, and Hamilton Gamble. McGirk retired in 1841 and was replaced by William Scott. Tompkins was forced to retire in 1845 when he reached the mandatory retirement age of sixty-five and was replaced by Priestly McBride. Gamble was left alone, although he remained a staunch supporter of the freedom suits and even wrote the dissenting opinion in the Missouri Dred Scott case.

Judge William Scott, author of the Dred Scott majority opinion, previously served on the supreme court of Missouri as a result of an appointment in 1841. Judge John Ryland had been appointed to the court in 1849 and was elected in 1850. The third judge was Chief Justice Hamilton Gamble, a prominent St. Louis lawyer who accepted an invitation from a nearly unanimous St. Louis Bar to run for the state supreme court. Gamble refused to campaign for the job, but he felt that it was his duty to make himself available for the position, especially because he had urged the change to judicial elections. A slaveholder, he was elected overwhelmingly; however, he also was a man who put principle above his own beliefs and was the court's lone dissenter in the Dred Scott case.

Hamilton Gamble

Another of the giants was Hamilton Rowan Gamble, born on November 29, 1798, in Winchester, Virginia. He was the seventh and youngest child born to Joseph and Anne Hamilton Gamble. In 1812, at the age of thirteen, Gamble began attending Hampden-Sidney College in Virginia. After leaving college, he studied law. By 1819, at the age of twenty, Gamble was licensed to practice law in Virginia, Tennessee, and Missouri.

Gamble came to St. Louis in 1818 to join the law firm of his brother Archibald, who was, at the time, a clerk for the Missouri Circuit Court. Archibald appointed his brother Hamilton a deputy circuit court clerk. Shortly after, Hamilton Gamble became prosecuting attorney of the circuit court of Howard County, Missouri.

Gamble lived briefly in St. Louis before moving to Howard County, Missouri, in 1819 where he worked as a lawyer. The next year he received an appointment as circuit attorney for the St. Louis Circuit Court. Gamble's older brother, Archibald, a clerk of the court, likely used his influence to help his brother obtain the appointment. Gamble developed a drinking problem during this time that almost ended his career. He resigned from his position in 1823 but was able to overcome his issue with alcohol, and in 1824 Governor Frederick Bates appointed Gamble secretary of state. Gamble moved to St. Charles, which at the time was the capital of Missouri.

Two years later, in 1826, Governor Bates died and Gamble resigned as secretary of state, returning to the practice of law in St. Louis, working chiefly on real estate cases where he made a substantial reputation.

In 1827, Gamble married Caroline J. Coalter from Columbia, South Carolina, who was the sister of the wife of Edward Bates. The Gambles had three children: Hamilton Gamble, Dr. David Gamble, and Mary Coalter Gamble.

Gamble was elected to the Missouri Supreme Court. While a member of the court, Gamble wrote the dissenting opinion in the important

Dred Scott case. This meant that he disagreed with the decision made by the majority of judges on the court. Gamble thought that Scott and his wife, Harriet, should have been awarded their freedom. He believed the court was undermining the judicial system by ignoring past decisions that freed slaves in similar cases. In 1846, Hamilton Gamble was elected to the  Missouri Supreme Court as a Whig, and he became chief justice. Justice Gamble continued service until his health forced him to resign in 1855, and in 1858 he moved for a time to Pennsylvania.

In early 1861 Gamble returned to Missouri at the insistence of his brother-in-law, Edward Bates, who was appointed attorney general in President Lincoln's administration. Bates wanted Gamble to attend the state convention being held to determine whether or not Missouri should secede. At the convention Gamble became the main proponent for Missouri to remain in the Union, and delegates elected him chairman of the committee on federal relations. In June 1861, Gamble was appointed provisional governor after Governor Claiborne Fox Jackson, a Southern sympathizer, fled the capital with fellow supporters. As provisional governor, Gamble remained committed to keeping Missouri from seceding from the Union, as well as to maintaining law and order. He sought to restore peace and issued special orders to kill guerrillas in Missouri. Guerrillas were civilian combatants who worked to sabotage Union military efforts. During the Civil War, Gamble supported a gradual system of emancipation rather than an immediate end to slavery.

Governor Claiborne Fox Jackson called for secession from the Union, but he was forcibly removed from office and fled the state in

1861. A state convention was called on January 21, 1861, to decide whether Missouri would secede from the United States or remain in the Union. The federal troops and the citizenry of St. Louis prevented any action to secede. At the age of sixty-three, Gamble was brought out of his Pennsylvania retirement and returned to St. Louis to become provisional governor of Missouri in July 1861, where he tried to keep Missouri on the path of remaining part of the Union while resisting federal control. During the Civil War, Gamble led the state through circumstances bordering on anarchy between Unionists and Secessionists within Missouri and from neighboring states, attempts by radicals within his own party to remove him as governor, and disagreements with generals in the Union Army that required President Lincoln's intervention. The correspondence between President Lincoln, Attorney General Edward Bates, and Governor Gamble sheds light on conditions in Missouri during the Civil War. Gamble's letters show his intense patriotism to the Union, but they also protest against unnecessary harshness and acts of repression on the part of federal authorities.

Gamble's exhausting work as governor, together with a broken arm he suffered in a fall on the ice at the executive mansion, led to a case of pneumonia, which resulted in his death in January 1864. Local memorials honored him more for his service as governor than for his efforts as a lawyer. The *Missouri Democrat* reported that Missouri militia members would wear badges of mourning for thirty days, and flags in all public buildings were flown at half mast. Rounds of artillery at Lucas Square fired every ten minutes during the funeral services. Members of Gamble's staff met and issued a proclamation regarding the order of the procession for his funeral, which was published and the public was invited to attend. Services were held at Second Presbyterian Church at Fifth and Walnut streets. Gamble is buried in Bellefontaine Cemetery in St. Louis beside his wife.

His wife, Caroline, and three children survived him, however, Caroline died before his estate was settled. Gamble's estate consisted mostly of personal property—$5,080.05; gold at Boatman's Savings

Institute—$20,000.00; currency at Boatman's Savings—$13,534.25; gold at L.A. Benoist & Co.—$500.00; currency at L.A. Benoist & Co.—$2,645.21; Mechanic's Bank Stock—$2,000.00; receipt of R. Homes—$10,000.00; railroad tax receipts—$1,231.77; promissory notes—$95,521.97; and interest on notes—$3,183.07, for a balance of $78,417.22.

Gamble left one slave, with a note in the probate file dated May 28, 1864, from son Hamilton Gamble acknowledging receipt from a Charles Gibson that his father bequeathed him one Negro woman named Gabriella and her three children, Louis, John, and Alexandra.

The final settlement indicated that $689.68 was divided between Sallie M. Gamble, executrix for Hamilton Gamble (son), Mary and Edgar Miller (daughter), and David Gamble.

A lot of debt, evident from notes in the file, apparently accumulated from Gibson paying the bills of the children (Hamilton, Mary, and David) or giving them money from the estate before it was settled. Eventually Hamilton, Mary, and David sued Gibson, with their petition stating that Gibson misused funds and/or used funds to his advantage. It looks like the court pulled in a "referee" to handle the dispute and everything was settled; however, a notation indicates that Gibson had to pay court costs involved with the suit.

Gamble had three streets (Hamilton, Rowan, and Gamble) and a school, Gamble School, named after him.

ALEXANDER HAMILTON

ALEXANDER HAMILTON WAS BORN IN PHILADELPHIA IN 1814 INTO A family of some social standing. His father, Hugh Hamilton, migrated to the United States from the Protestant part of Northern Ireland and settled in Philadelphia, where he married Sarah Kane, who died when Alexander was six years old. Alexander was admitted to the Pennsylvania Bar in 1831 and moved to Missouri for unknown reasons. According to the *Encyclopedia of the History of St. Louis*, written in 1899, before moving to Missouri he had the good fortune to have married Miss Julia Keen. Julia's maternal uncles were distinguished U.S. Navy officers. Her first cousin was James Lawrence, who will be forever remembered for shouting, "Don't give up the ship, boys," from the Revolution. Alexander and Julia had two daughters—Anna, who married Lewis Bailey of Boston, and Virginia, who married Theodore Forster of St. Louis. Both daughters lived in St. Louis at the time of Alexander's death on October 27, 1882.

Being of Northern Irish ancestry, Alexander could no longer be a member of the Church of England, so he became an Episcopalian and by the time of his death was one of the oldest members of the Christ Church congregation in St. Louis.

Hamilton was originally appointed to the circuit court bench in 1847 by Governor John Edwards. He was reappointed by Governor Austin A. King and then elected in 1849. He continued to be reelected until 1857 and was an acknowledged antislavery advocate. He replaced John Krumm on the bench, who interestingly was the circuit judge at the time the Dred Scott case was originally filed in 1846. Since Hamilton replaced Krumm in 1847, Krumm had no significant part in the Dred Scott case for which Hamilton will be forever remembered.

While he was not on the bench, he was generally considered among the best of the lawyers, along with the likes of Bates, Barton, Geyer, Gamble, Spalding, Lawless, Field, Bowlin, and Primm.

He was among the St. Louis lawyers who established the St. Louis

Law Library, now atop the Civil Courts Building. During his later years, he was the attraction for most of the young lawyers in the area. Hamilton admitted the likes of Thomas Finney to the bar in 1849 and as late as 1854, David R. Barclay was known to be "reading" law under Hamilton.

In 1880, St. Louis Judge Thomas Gantt suggested to Hamilton that he run for the supreme court, which by that time was an elected position. Gantt almost guaranteed Hamilton's election, if he would let his supporters put his name up for election. Hamilton, however, said that he thought he was too old to serve. This may have been the earliest consideration of some sort of mandatory retirement age for judges in Missouri.

Matthias McGirk

One of the first judges in Missouri was Matthias McGirk, a contemporary of the Bartons. His judicial colleagues were J. D. Cook and John R. Jones. They were appointed in 1820. Judge McGirk was born in 1790, in Tennessee, and reached St. Louis around 1814. In 1816 he was author of the bill to introduce the common law into Missouri, and he framed other important bills while a member of the legislature. In 1827 he removed to Montgomery County, and there married a Miss Talbot. In 1841 he retired from the bench, devoting himself to agriculture. He was not a brilliant jurist but had practical sense, a retentive memory, and an admirable style, both as conversationalist and writer. In politics he was a Whig. Little information is obtainable about Andrew and Isaac McGirk, relatives of the preceding, who also practiced law in St. Louis. Isaac died in 1830.

John D. Cook, Judge McGirk's associate on the bench, was a member of the state constitutional convention, and a jurist of excellence. When Judge E. S. Thomas was removed from the circuit court, Judge Cook was appointed. He presided there many years and was a noted *nisi prius* judge. He had great ability but was too indolent to take a commanding place. Judge Cook was always a pleasant companion and widely known for his benevolence and friendliness to younger members of the profession.

While he was in private practice, McGirk argued a number of cases in the U.S. Supreme Court, including: *Chouteau v. Eckhart*, 43 U.S. 344 (1844); *Mackay v. Dillon*, 45 U.S. 421 (1846); *Missouri v. Iowa*, 48 U.S. 660 (1849); *Bissell v. Penrose*, 49 U.S. 317 (1849); *Mills v. Stoddard*, 49 U.S. 345 (1850); *Mills v. St. Clair County*, 49 U.S. 569 (1850); *Landes v. Brant*, 51 U.S. 348 (1850); *Easton v. Salisbury*, 62 U.S. 426 (1858); *Fenn v. Holme*, 62 U.S. 481 (1858); *Berthold v. McDonald*, 63 U.S. 334 (1859).

McGirk Street, crossing Twelfth Street, was named for Matthias.

JOHN RYLAND

WHILE WILLIAM SCOTT WROTE THE MAJORITY OPINION IN *SCOTT V. Emerson* for the Missouri Supreme Court, it was John Ryland who joined with him and reversed forty years of Missouri precedent.

Ryland was born in Virginia on November 2, 1797, the oldest of seven children born to Joseph and Rose Amaya Ryland. The family moved to Richmond County, Kentucky, and his father died shortly after leaving Mrs. Ryland with her seven children and a small farm. John Ryland particularly enjoyed ancient history, and while he and his brothers were out in the field, John would relate all the wondrous deeds of Julius Caesar and Hannibal. His mother decided that his knowledge of ancient history was of no particular value in cultivating the farm, so she sent him to Forest Hill Academy in Marion County, Kentucky, where he became fluent in Latin. Ryland opened a school and at one time had as many as 120 students. He read law in Kentucky under Judge Hartman and although he was licensed in Kentucky, he did not practice until he moved to Missouri in 1819. Ryland settled in Howard County, where he established what was described as a lucrative practice. He practiced law in Pettis, Randolph, Ray, and Saline counties as well.

In 1830, Ryland was appointed chief judge of the sixth circuit and held that position for eighteen years. When he became a circuit judge, he moved to Lafayette County, where he lived for the rest of his life.

In 1848, Ryland was appointed to the Missouri Supreme Court, and stayed on the bench until 1857, when he returned to private practice until he died in December 1873.

Ryland's contribution to Missouri was not limited to his legal pursuits. During the Civil War he had been captured by the Confederates and was involved in a prisoner exchange.

Beginning in the spring of 1861, Ebenezer Magoffin traveled to Jefferson City and offered his services to Governor Claiborne Jackson, who was getting ready to issue a call for 50,000 volunteers to stop the federal troops from occupying Missouri. Magoffin and Major Thomas

Stapleton started recruiting a militia for Governor Jackson in the Boonville area. Jackson's ill-trained and ill-equipped militia was easily defeated, and he retreated to Neosho, Missouri, where he set up a temporary state capital. Magoffin continued to recruit for the Missouri militia but was captured by the federal troops near Lexington, Missouri. He was suspected of killing a federal soldier and was held. Fortunately for Magoffin, the Missouri militia defeated the federal troops at the Battle of Lexington. In a prisoner exchange, Magoffin was exchanged for former Missouri Governor Austin A. King and former Missouri Supreme Court Judge John Ryland, prisoners of Magoffin's son, Captain Elijah Magoffin. History does not tell us how Ryland had been taken prisoner by the Missouri militia.

In politics, Ryland was a Democrat and sided with the Union during the Civil War.

Ryland married twice, first to Martha Barnett on October 29, 1818, while he was still in Kentucky. Ryland and Martha had six children, James, Erasmus, William, Cacius Tacitus, John E. Ryland, and Juliet Martha. Ryland's first wife died in 1833, and he then married Elizabeth Buford in 1835, by whom he fathered twelve children, Elizabeth, Rosanna, Gabriella, Margaret, Caroline, Mary, Catherine, Simean, Xenophon, Manville, Joseph, and Richard. Elizabeth died in 1884. Of his eighteen children, three of them became practicing lawyers.

William Scott

Scott was born in Warrenton, Virginia, in June 1804. He was admitted to the Virginia Bar but did not practice much in Virginia. He moved to Missouri in the fall of 1826, to Old Franklin in Howard County. He was not very successful as a lawyer because of his quick temper. In fact, opposing counsel found it easy to get Scott angry to the point that he was so distracted by losing his temper in court that the opposition beat him easily. Because of this, his many friends who appreciated his knowledge of the law appointed him judge of the Ninth Circuit in 1835, covering Franklin, Gasconade, Jefferson, and St. Francis counties. He bought a small farm, about four miles south of Union.

Scott was a large man, weighing approximately 250 pounds. It was difficult for him to walk any distance without getting winded. He was terrified of drowning because he couldn't swim. Because of the relatively large area of his circuit, he traveled often, frequently fording creeks. As now, Missouri was notorious for its lack of decent bridges. When he rode across a creek, Scott would always drag his feet through the water, for fear of falling off his horse. He was not a good public speaker and always avoided speaking before large crowds.

In 1835, Scott married Elizabeth Dixon of Cole County, who bore him six children. He was such a great judge that many lawyers would travel to his court to watch him. After he was appointed to the Missouri Supreme Court, he moved to Cole County and spent the remainder of his life on a small farm a few miles west of Jefferson City. Scott died on May 18, 1862, at the age of fifty-eight.

Scott had a great sense of justice, to the extent that he would never permit what he perceived to be wrong perpetrated. In one instance, when the sheriff was selling a farm under execution to satisfy a judgment belonging to a poor resident, the highest bid for the land, which was well worth five hundred dollars, was a mere twenty dollars. The judge, learning of this, stopped the sale and declared that as long as he was the judge, the household was not going to be sold for such a paltry sum.

It was the custom of the supreme court that each judge would read aloud the decisions that he had written. In one case, while Judge Scott was reading an opinion in which a guardian had defrauded his ward, Scott rose from his seat and declared that, in his opinion, the scoundrel deserved to be thrown into the halter. It is this sense of "justice" that may have drawn him to favor the concept of the freedom suits, and the rule of "once free, always free."

Although Scott wasn't necessarily opposed to the Union, he was perceived to be a sympathizer of the Confederacy.

While he had a good memory regarding most matters, Scott had a terrible memory for names. One story circulated that he ran into an acquaintance on the street, whose name he couldn't remember. He asked the gentleman how he spelled his last name stating that Scott and his wife differed on the correct spelling of the man's last name. The acquaintance said his name was spelled the same as everyone else's, S-M-I-T-H.[53]

George Tompkins

George Tompkins was born in Caroline County, Virginia, in March 1780 to Benjamin Tompkins and Elizabeth Goodloe Tompkins. He was the second youngest of thirteen children whose ancestors were among the earliest settlers in Virginia. Tompkins's family owned extensive property in Virginia worked by a large number of slaves. Tobacco was the primary product, which was shipped to England. There doesn't seem to be a great deal of information as to when he left Virginia. Tompkins first moved to Kentucky for six or seven years as a schoolteacher and studied law part time. Given his background as part of a large slave-owning family, there is little that explains his siding with Winny in *Winny v. Whitesides.*

Tompkins moved to St. Louis and took over a school run by a man named Rotchford, who opened the first English school in St. Louis in 1804. Tompkins rented a room on the north side of Market Street, between Second and Third, for his pupils, and studied law at the same time. Tompkins was so well thought of by students and parents that when he announced he was closing his school to practice law full time, parents did whatever they could to dissuade him. Finally, in order to convince his students and their families that he was serious about going from school teacher to lawyer, he sold all of his school furniture, books, and the school house. Once he no longer had the physical tools to run a school, his students' families accepted his decision.

In 1816, he moved to Old Franklin in Howard County, Missouri, northwest of Columbia and started his practice. He was twice elected to the territorial legislature, which was then in St. Charles.

When J. R. Jones died, leaving a vacancy on the Missouri Supreme Court, Tompkins was appointed to the bench in 1824 and held the position until 1845 when he was forced to retire by a constitutional provision that prohibited any person from holding office after age sixty-five. At the time he was put on the Missouri Supreme Court, Matthias McGirk and Rufus Pettibone were already on the bench. After he retired, Tompkins moved to his farm near Jefferson City, Missouri.

In *Reminiscences of the Bench and Bar of Missouri*, William V. N. Bay gave this description of Tompkins:

> *At times he was irritable on the bench, and would frequently interrupt counsel in their argument with some odd remark or sarcastic inquiry. He dressed very plain, but never could tolerate slovenliness in others. A lawyer from one of the south eastern counties, by the name of Mendell, was once engaged in an argument in his court, when Judge Tompkins interrupted him, near the time of the adjourning hour, by saying "Mr. Mendell, it is impossible for this court to see any law through as dirty a shirt as you have on and this court will now adjourn until 10:00 tomorrow morning to give you the opportunity to change your linens.*

Tompkins died on April 7, 1846, on his farm near Jefferson City. His wife, Elizabeth Lientz Tompkins, had died in 1836, and their only son, William B. Tompkins, died at the age of one in 1830. Tompkins left no family.

FREEDOM SUITS

GIVEN THAT ALL OF THE PLAINTIFFS WERE SLAVES, HOW DID THEY LEARN of the possibility of gaining their freedom through the courts? The second question then becomes, how did they find lawyers willing to accept these cases? And third, who paid the cost? There was no legal aid in Missouri, nor were there civil rights law groups like the ACLU.[54]

In the 1810s and 1820s, the success rates of the freedom suits dramatically increased, providing real incentive for pursuing freedom in the courts. But the very early suits do not provide much information on their origins, beginning with Marie Jean Scypion.

Slaves in the St. Louis area had considerably more "freedom" in the sense that they had the ability to communicate freely with others. For instance, a slave would conduct his or her chores off the owner's property. So if a slave was going to the market or down to the levee, he or she would have the opportunity to hear what was going on in the community and to talk with their counterparts. The slaves would therefore learn of the freedom suits and which lawyers were involved. Certainly by the early 1820s, the number of freedom suits had grown.

Suing for your freedom was not without hardships. The simplest way for slave owners to thwart a freedom suit was to ship the slave out of the jurisdiction of the court, selling the slave "down the river." Eventually the courts and the slaves' lawyers got smart enough to get the court to order that the owner not remove the slave from the jurisdiction of the court. The owners got around this by selling or transferring the slave to someone else, who would then move the slave "down the river." Accordingly, the slaves' lawyers and the courts would order the owner to post a bond, normally extremely high, to guarantee the owner would not do something incredibly stupid. Another alternative, if the owner would not or could not post the bond, was to order the slave be put into the custody of the sheriff, who would be ordered to rent out the slave to whomever he could find, for whatever he could get, and to hold the "rental" for the court to decide later. This last alternative led to a lot of physical hardships on the slaves. The sheriffs normally were not particularly concerned about the welfare of the slaves. They would not see that the slaves were cared for either in the jail or in the rental. A lot of letters were written to the lawyers by their clients about the terrible treatment given by the sheriffs.

Of particular interest is that even after the Dred Scott case in 1848, the freedom suits continued, although the results of the vast majority of these cases are unknown.

The difference in attitudes within families over slavery is also evident in the freedom suits. For instance, Dred Scott was originally brought to Missouri as a slave by Peter Blow and his family. After the U.S. Supreme Court decision, Dred and his family were "bought" by Taylor Blow of St. Louis on May 26, 1857, and freed.

In almost every instance, the question in the trial was whether the "owner" voluntarily took the "slave" into the free territory for any length of time. If the Missouri court found the move into the free territory to be voluntary and that some residence was established, the slaves were freed. If the trip into free territory was involuntary, or merely passing through, the slaves were not freed. So, in *Scott v. Emerson*, the question arose whether Emerson voluntarily moved into free territory or was he ordered to go by the military.

The lot of the freed slaves "improved" in St. Louis by the beginning of the Civil War. Cyprian Clamorgan, a free black man who had accumulated considerable wealth and property, observed that free blacks had accumulated several million dollars, and they knew who had the money and that, although they could not vote, they knew who their friends were. Clamorgan is still remembered with "Clamorgan Alley" in the Laclede's Landing area in downtown St. Louis.

DRED SCOTT

IT IS WELL KNOWN THAT DRED SCOTT ULTIMATELY LOST HIS BID FOR freedom through the courts, and Justice Roger Taney delivered the ultimate insult in the U.S. Supreme Court by declaring that Dred Scott and his family were not "persons" within the meaning of the U.S. Constitution. Few people, however, know that twelve white men voted in favor of the Scotts when the issue was tried in 1850. So it might be helpful to review the Scotts' trip through the judicial system.

Dred Scott was born to slave parents in Virginia in 1799. By 1830, Peter Blow had settled his family of four sons, three daughters, and six slaves to St. Louis. This was after having moved from Virginia to Alabama, to attempt farming near Huntsville, and, when farming failed, a move from Alabama to Missouri. In St. Louis, Peter Blow undertook the running of a boarding house, the Jefferson Hotel. Within a year, though, Peter Blow's wife, Elizabeth, died and on June 23, 1832, Peter Blow passed away.

When the Blow family moved to St. Louis, they sold Dred Scott to Dr. John Emerson, a military doctor stationed at Jefferson Barracks. Over the next twelve years, Scott accompanied Emerson to two military posts in Illinois and Wisconsin Territory, where slavery was prohibited. During these twelve years, Scott married Harriet Robinson, and they had two children. There was a suggestion in a newspaper account at the time that Dred had been married prior to Harriet, but little is known of this earlier marriage. In 1842, Emerson, his wife, Irene, and Dred and Harriet Scott moved back to St. Louis. Emerson died, and Irene Emerson hired out Dred, Harriet, and their children to work for other families in St. Louis.

The Blow children remained in St. Louis after the deaths of their parents and became well established in the city's society through marriage to prominent families. Charlotte Taylor Blow married Joseph Charless Jr., in November 1831. His father had established the first newspaper west of the Mississippi River and had been a leading opponent of slavery while editor. Joseph, Jr., operated a wholesale drug and paint store, Charless & Company (later Charless, Blow & Company, when brothers-in-law Henry Taylor Blow and Taylor Blow became partners). Martha Ella Blow married attorney Charles Drake in 1835. Drake is better known in history for his role in the creation of Missouri's 1865 Constitution. As a leader of the Radical Republican Party after the Civil War, Drake was determined to punish those considered Southern sympathizers; the constitution he helped author took away many of their rights, including enfranchisement. Peter Ethelrod Blow married Eugenie LaBeaume in 1838. She was from an old French banking family; her oldest brother was a wealthy businessman who, in partnership with Blow, formed Peter E. Blow & Company. She had two other brothers; one was the St. Louis County sheriff for a time in the 1840s, and the other, Charles Edmund LaBeaume, was a St. Louis attorney who played an important role in Dred Scott's freedom suits. All of these St. Louis connections proved significant to Blow's practice and life.

In 1846, Dred and Harriet sued Mrs. Emerson for their freedom in the state circuit court. During the course of the litigation, once the federal part of the suit got going, the Emerson/Sanford family was represented by a group of lawyers—Hugh A. Garland, Henry S. Geyer, George W. Goode, Reverdy Johnson, and Lyman D. Norris. Dred's family was also represented by a team of lawyers—Samuel M. Bay, Montgomery Blair, George Ticknor Curtis, Alexander P. Field, Roswell M. Field, and David N. Hall. Frances B. Murdoch, who had moved to St. Louis from Alton, Illinois, in 1841, originally represented the Scott family. He probably was connected with the Scott family through John Anderson, who was the minister at the Second African Baptist Church where Harriet attended in St. Louis. For some reason, Murdoch moved to California in 1847, before the Scott case came to trial.

At this point, the children of Peter Blow started providing financial and legal assistance to the Scott family. Charlotte Blow Charless had requested her brother-in-law, Charles Drake, to take over the case when

Murdoch left. Drake was the widower of Martha Ella Blow, and after she died, his sister-in-law, Elizabeth Blow, cared for their two children, which kept Drake in close contact with the Blow family. Although the record is unclear as to whether Drake actually appeared in court for the Scotts, we know he did take the depositions and prepare the case for the trial. He moved to Cincinnati in June 1847, leaving the Scotts without an attorney again. At this point, Samuel Mansfield Bay, a New Yorker by birth, became the Scotts' attorney of record. Bay was the attorney for the Bank of Missouri, which was owned by Joseph Charless Jr., who was the husband of Charlotte Blow Charless. We now have the merger of the Charless and the Blow families supporting the Scotts.

In 1847, the circuit court ruled in favor of Mrs. Emerson. The case was presided over by Judge Alexander Hamilton, who had replaced the proslavery Judge John Krumm. Hamilton was generally sympathetic toward the freedom suits. At this time, Missouri precedent, thanks to the *Winny v. Whitesides* case, was clearly on the side of the Scotts. George Goode represented Mrs. Emerson at the trial. One of the key pieces of the testimony involved Samuel Russell of St. Louis, who testified that he had hired Dred and Harriet Scott from Irene Emerson and paid her father, Alexander Sanford, for their services. On cross-examination, however, Goode revealed that it was Russell's wife, Adeline, who had made the arrangements to hire the Scotts from Irene Emerson and that all that Samuel Russell had done was pay the rental money to Sanford. Judge Hamilton ruled that Samuel Russell's testimony was stricken as hearsay and there was therefore no admissible evidence that Irene Emerson ever claimed to hold the Scotts as slaves. Because of the technicality, the jury was instructed to return a verdict against the Scotts, which it did. The problem was that the jury did not hear evidence to prove "once free, always free." They simply didn't hear enough testimony to prove that Irene Emerson ever claimed or held Dred and Harriet Scott as her slaves.

The Scotts' lawyers moved for a new trial and filed an appeal to the Missouri Supreme Court. While the appeal was pending, Judge

Hamilton granted the motion for a new trial. So in June 1848, Judge William Scott of the Missouri Supreme Court issued an order stating that because the motion for a new trial had been granted, there was nothing for the supreme court to rule on.

In March 1848, before the new trial took place, Irene Emerson had the St. Louis sheriff take charge of the Scott family to hire them out, which he did until March 1857. Beginning in 1851, the Scotts were hired out to Charles LaBeaume, for whom they worked for about seven years. In 1849 or 1850, Mrs. Emerson moved to Springfield, Massachusetts, where she married Dr. Calvin Chaffee in November 1850. Chaffee was an abolitionist and apparently was unaware of his wife's involvement in the Scotts' suit.

Also before the second trial, John Sanford, Mrs. Emerson's brother, had pretty much taken over managing his sister's affairs, including possession of the Scotts. This time, the Scotts' lawyers were Alexander P. Field and David N. Hall. Sanford had by this time completely taken over the widow Emerson's affairs and retained Hugh A. Garland and Lyman D. Norris for the defense.

The long delay in the retrial of the Scotts was caused in part by the court's heavy docket, the fire of 1849, and the cholera epidemic. The second trial began in 1849, Judge Hamilton again presiding. No one seemed to figure out how Irene kept the fact that she owned a slave from her new husband. This time the deposition of Adeline Russell was included, which showed that she had made the arrangements with Irene Emerson personally to hire out the Scotts. Samuel Russell appeared again to testify that he paid Mrs. Emerson for the hiring of the slaves. The technicality that cost the Scotts their freedom in 1847 had now been overcome. With this new testimony, Judge Hamilton instructed the jury that they should return a verdict for the plaintiff, an early example of a directed verdict.

What is often overlooked is that the jury consisted of twelve white males, some of whom were slave owners. There is not much known about these twelve men. John Morris was a carpenter born in

Pennsylvania in 1817; Calvin Harris was a salesman born in Missouri in 1806; Robert West was a bartender, possibly working for J. B. Bogert, born in Maryland in 1826; and Charles W. Granthan was born in Virginia in 1830. Of the rest, C. H. Vosburg, William Syphert, H. S. Taylor, L Wyland, A. H. Foster, N. W. Stenchum, and D. Welsh, we know nothing other than their names.

Dred and Harriet Scott Were Free People

EMERSON'S LAWYERS ASKED FOR A NEW TRIAL, WHICH WAS DENIED, AND they then appealed to the Missouri Supreme Court. By this time, the antislavery judges that ruled in favor of Winny in *Winny v. Whitesides* had been replaced by two new judges who were proslavery. The new judges were looking for a case to overrule what had been almost forty years of precedent in Missouri. These new judges, William Scott and John Ryland, rendered the court's decision on March 22, 1852. Justice Scott wrote the opinion with Ryland concurring. Hamilton Gamble wrote the dissent. Scott and Ryland concluded that Missouri no longer had to recognize the laws of other states which were in opposition to Missouri laws. Illinois was a free state, Missouri was a slave state. So Missouri would no longer defer to other states. If a slave sued in Missouri, only Missouri law would apply. Gamble urged that the issue of comity had been long established in Missouri, and that a number of Southern slave states had followed the Missouri rule—if the owner voluntarily took the slave to a free state, the slave was free. Scott, Ryland, and Gamble all recognized that the Scott decision was an outright reversal of the Missouri law; however, Scott and Ryland gave no reason why the precedent should be abandoned, except that it would no longer be followed. The only reference to *Winny v. Whitesides* was in a footnote, which read that this decision "Overrules 1 Mo. R. 479; 2 Mo. R 19 and 36; 3 Mo R. 194, 270, 400, 4 Mo. R. 350 and 592." 1 Mo. R. 479 was the official cite for *Winny v. Whitesides*.

The Blow family made the decision that they could no longer

financially support the Scotts' pursuit. The new attorney representing the Scotts, Alexander Field, had moved to Louisiana, and Charles LaBeaume, who had hired the Scotts from Mrs. Emerson, talked Roswell Field into taking over the case.

In November 1853, Field filed his new suit in the federal courts, this time including the Scotts' daughters Eliza and Lizzie. John Sanford, Irene Emerson's brother, probably to avoid embarrassing his sister who had married an abolitionist, now claimed ownership of the Scott family, so he was the defendant. His lawyer was Hugh Garland. Judge Robert Wells, the federal judge, held, during the preliminary stages, that the Scotts were citizens and had standing to file the suit. The case was submitted on an agreed statement of facts in 1854. Judge Wells ruled in favor of Sanford, generally following the new Missouri rule that once the Scotts were brought back into Missouri, they became slaves again. Field appealed to the U.S. Supreme Court and arranged to have Montgomery Blair, a St. Louis lawyer living in Washington, argue the Dred Scott case before the Supreme Court. Blair had a lot of political muscle in Washington, was abolitionist, a close friend of Thomas Hart Benton, and a leader in the Missouri Free Soil Movement. Gamaliel Bailey, the editor of the antislavery *National Era*, agreed to underwrite the court costs of the appeal. Oral arguments began in February 1856. In May 1856, the Supreme Court asked for the case to be re-argued in December, and the following year, the U.S. Supreme Court held that the Scotts were still slaves. Interestingly, however, seven of the nine justices wrote separate opinions.

After the U.S. Supreme Court decision, Irene Emerson's abolitionist second husband, Dr. Calvin Chaffee, by now a Massachusetts congressman, found out that his wife owned the Scotts, who may have been the most famous slaves in America. It is not known how he found out, or what he had to say to his bride when he did, but, in February 1857, shortly after the Supreme Court decision, Sanford transferred ownership of the Scott family to Taylor Blow in St. Louis. On May 26, 1857, Dred and Harriet Scott formally appeared in the St. Louis Circuit

Court and were formally emancipated by Taylor Blow. Most fittingly, Judge Alexander Hamilton approved the paperwork. Dred Scott took a job as a porter at the Barnum Hotel at Second and Walnut streets in St. Louis. The family lived off of Carr Street. Harriet took in laundry, which Dred delivered when he was not working at the hotel. Dred did not live to enjoy his freedom long. On September 17, 1857, less than four months after being emancipated, he died of tuberculosis. Harriet died on June 17, 1876. She was buried at the Greenwood Cemetery in St. Louis County. A front-page article in *Frank Leslie's Illustrated Newspaper*

dated Saturday, June 27, 1857, contains descriptions and illustrations of Dred Scott and his family based on an interview conducted with him and Harriet.

Dred Scott was described by the reporter as "a pure-blooded African, perhaps fifty years of age, with a shrewd, intelligent, good-natured face, of rather light frame, being not more than five feet six inches high." On the second page of the article, the reporter remarked that "Dred Scott, as might be supposed, is quite a humble man but nevertheless a real hero, moving about the streets of St. Louis. He attracts a great deal of attention from strangers, and as many stop to converse with him, they rarely fail to contribute something to his wants. He employs himself in carrying to and from the clothes his wife washes, and waiting, as opportunity offers, upon gentlemen at the hotels." The reporter also stated that Harriet Scott was Scott's second wife and that together they had four children, two sons and two daughters. The sons were dead at the time of the interview.

The Dred Scott case is the most famous and best known of the "freedom suits," and to some extent one of the most precedential. Had the judges of the Missouri Supreme Court not changed, had the court followed established Missouri law, the Scotts would have remained free after the Circuit Court jury ruled in their favor. Justice Taney's infamous decision would never have been written. We might likely never have heard any more about Dred and Harriet Scott. But the makeup of the Missouri Supreme Court did change. Justice Taney did write his decision. And the Dred Scott decisions unquestionably played a part in the beginnings of the Civil War. In legal circles, there is a saying that bad facts frequently make bad law. In the Scott case, bad judges made bad law.[55]

Marie Jean Scypion

THE EARLIEST SUIT, OF WHICH RECORDS HAVE BEEN FOUND, INVOLVED THE descendants of Marie Scypion. While the suit was originally filed in Missouri in 1806, its long path did not end until the U.S. Supreme Court ruled that it did not have jurisdiction to hear the appeal to it. This case could have made a fantastic movie, involving courage, heroism, heroes and villains, kindness, evil, and lasting through three generations and more than thirty-three years of perseverance. Given all of the family generations involved, the courts, the social infighting within the St. Louis aristocracy, the public outcry over the oligarchy, the general public's views in the St. Louis community about slavery, perhaps all of this confusion was caused because no one was completely clear as to the meaning of the old Spanish laws. Plus, the territorial laws of 1805 allowed impoverished slaves to sue as a poor person.

The secretary of state's website describes Marie's efforts to gain her freedom as follows:

> *Although it was not unusual for a case to drag on for several years, one family's struggle lasted three decades. In 1805, the children of Afro-Indian slave Marie Jean Scypion filed the first suit for freedom in Missouri with the Territorial Superior Court. Indian slavery was common in territorial Missouri until Spanish officials ordered an end to the practice in 1769. Unhappy slaveholders resisted the order, but some slaves, including Scypion's descendants, saw in it a chance for freedom. Scypion's children asserted in their petition that Marie Jean's mother was Indian, and that ancestry, the plaintiffs argued, precluded their enslavement. The initial judgment in their favor was reversed in a later trial and over the next thirty years, Scypion's descendants, most notably her daughters Marguerite, Celeste, and Catiche continued to press their claim. Encouraged by the Missouri General Assembly's passage of a state statute allowing persons held in slavery to sue for their freedom, Marguerite renewed her claim in 1825 and filed suit against her owner Pierre Chouteau, Sr., in the St. Louis Circuit Court.*

Although the judgment and subsequent appeal to the Missouri Supreme Court went against Marguerite, her attorney's persistence brought about a review of the case in 1834 and a new trial was ordered. After a change of venue to St. Charles County, and then Jefferson County, and delays on the part of Chouteau's legal counsel, the case finally came to trial on November 8, 1836. The jury's unanimous decision in favor of the plaintiffs withstood appeals by the defense to the State and U.S. Supreme Courts, thus officially ending the practice of Indian slavery in Missouri.

Marie Jean Scypion, sometimes confused with her daughter and inappropriately referred to as Marguerite Scypion, was generally accepted to have been born in the 1740s near what is today Fort Chartres, Illinois. Her mother was Marie or Mariette, a Natchez Indian woman, who had been captured during the Indian wars and sold into slavery. Her father was a black slave named Scypion who either died at Prairie du Rocher or was taken to New Orleans by his owner. As to whether Marie and Scypion were owned by the same person is not known. Marie was of a reddish-brown complexion and wore her curly hair in the French fashion under her handkerchief.

Marie Jean was owned by a French priest named Guyon, who gave her to his cousin, Madame Marie Boisset. Madame Boisset's daughter, Marie Louise, married Joseph Tayon, and subsequently inherited Marie Jean. In 1769, while the Spanish owned the Louisiana Territory, Governor General Alejandro O'Reilly ordered that the practice of Indian slavery be terminated. Intended as an effort to gather some favor with the numerous Indian tribes in the territory, the order met with a storm of protests from the Indian slave owners in the territory. O'Reilly's decision was not entirely altruistic. The Osage Indians had been a source of constant threats to the Spanish inhabitants of St. Louis and Upper Louisiana. They would regularly raid the fur traders and trappers, and O'Reilly's decision was in part due to his desire to maintain some sort of peace with the Indians. Because of the unrest among the slave owners, the Spanish authorities agreed to allow the residents to keep their Indian slaves until the policy could be reviewed by the Spanish crown. But the slave owners were prohibited from selling their Indian slaves until some decision could be reached.

After Marie Jean was brought to St. Louis, she had three daughters, Celeste, Catiche, and Marguerite. History does not give us any certainty as to their father. After Celeste and Catiche were born, Madam Tayon put the girls in the custody of her daughters, Helene Chevalier and Marie Louise Chauvin. Marie Jean, though, remained in the Tayon household as a cook and housekeeper.

After Marie Boisset-Tayon's death, Mr. Tayon moved in with the Pierre Chouteau family. Chouteau was one of the wealthiest people in St. Louis and a large slaveholder who fiercely defended the practice. Pierre was the brother of Auguste Chouteau and had been appointed U.S. agent for Indian Affairs, by Thomas Jefferson, which helped expand his fur trading business with the Indians, particularly the Osage. He had negotiated the Osage Treaty of 1808, under which the Osage agreed to sell large portions of their land in Missouri and Arkansas to settlers for annual tribute payments.

In 1799, Joseph Tayon attempted to sell Marie Jean and her three daughters, but Tayon's daughters refused to return Celeste and Catiche. The family tried to resolve their differences as to claims to Marie Jean's daughters in the Spanish courts without conclusion. Zenon Trudeau, the Upper Louisiana lieutenant governor, held the position that Indian slaves could not be sold legally, with O'Reilly's 1769 order still in place.

Then came along 1803 and the Louisiana Purchase. Joseph Tayon sought permission from the new commandant, Captain Amos Stoddard, to sell Marie Jean's daughters. Tayon's daughters again thwarted their father's attempt to reclaim Marie's daughters by raising the issue that Marie was Indian, so Celeste, Catiche, and Marguerite could not be sold. The family engaged in a bit of *Dallas* family infighting, and eventually Lieutenant Governor Stoddard ordered that none of the girls could be sold until the soon-to-be-established territorial court had a chance to untangle the mess. The political intrigue that followed between the Chouteau brothers and local government officials, who still did not know what the laws were or were going to be, would equal the best that the political stage had to offer in twentieth- and twenty-first-century America. One of the curious facts of this litigation and family fighting is the realization that it was the first of several "freedom suits" where the family of "owners" fought over the slaveriness of the plaintiffs.

In October 1805, Celeste and Catiche filed for a writ of habeas corpus. Their lawyer was most likely Isaac Darnielle, one of the earliest practicing attorneys in Missouri. This was the beginning of the suit about which we started writing some pages ago. The dysfunctional Tayon family feud continued. Eventually the territorial judges, John B. C. Lucas and Rufus Easton, freed Celeste and Catiche. Easton and Lucas based their decision upon the affidavits from Madame Chevalier and her brother-in-law attesting that Celeste and Catiche were free Indians living voluntarily with them. Five days later, another writ was filed on behalf of Marguerite, Marie Jean's third daughter. With little to no precedent on which to base decision, Lucas and Easton ordered Francois Tayon to release all three women.

Lucas and Easton were charting new legal territory. St. Louis was now in American territory. What credence or authority should they give the old Spanish law, the old Spanish bans on Indian slavery? These judges used a combination of common sense and a certain amount of deference to popular opinion, which in St. Louis was generally antislavery. The plutocracy, of which the Chouteaus and other large slaveholding families were a part, were trying to protect their investments.

Joseph Tayon was not a gracious loser. For at the next session of the Territorial Superior Court, he tried to get an arrest warrant for the Scypion family. Lucas and Easton declined to authorize the arrest of Celeste and Catiche but ordered Tayon to post a $4,000 bond to ensure that he did not remove the girls from the court's jurisdiction. That was no small sum. Pierre Chouteau and merchant Bernard Pratte posted the bond for Tayon. We are not sure if this was a cash bond or a surety, by which they guaranteed to pay the amount of the bond if Tayon defaulted and took the girls out of the jurisdiction. It is more likely the latter. While the order did not name Marguerite, Pierre Chouteau, with whom Marguerite still lived, turned her over to Tayon. Lucas and Easton again ruled for the Scypion women, but in an apparent attempt to extricate themselves from the political turmoil, gave Tayon one month to file a separate suit to establish any legal right or claim he might have to the Scypion women.

The jury trial began in St. Louis on May 19, 1806, and lasted two days. When the jury elected Pierre Chouteau's brother-in-law, James Morrison, jury foreman, the Scypions knew things were going badly. And they did. The jury found that the women were black slaves. Darnielle immediately asked for a new trial and a rehearing, which were refused. Less than a month later, Tayon sold Marguerite, and her children—Antoine and Elizabeth—Catiche and her children—Carmelite and son—and Celeste's son, Paul, to Pierre Chouteau for $1,142.

Public sentiment was very much against the jury verdict. After the sale, one of Tayon's daughters filed suit to regain custody of at least some of the Scypions. The suit dragged on for several years, and ultimately Pierre Chouteau paid the Tayon daughters an unknown sum and settled the case.

These events did not dim the Scypions' determination. When the Missouri Legislature enacted the 1824 statutes, another lawyer, not Darnielle, filed another suit in 1825. This suit was denied by the circuit court, but on May 15, 1826, Judge George Tompkins of the Missouri Supreme Court ordered the case to proceed in accord with the 1824 statute. The court also ordered the circuit court to appoint lawyers for the Scypions, who were suing as poor persons. The circuit court appointed Isaac McGirk and Hamilton B. Gamble as the girls' lawyers. There were, in fact, several separate suits going on at the same time, all involving the Scypion women, Tayon, and Chouteau. Although the suits were separate, the women and their lawyers coordinated all their actions and strategies.

Chouteau was not a good loser as a litigant. On April 1, 1825, he beat Catiche and confined her for thirty days. Catiche and the others responded by filing separate counts charging Chouteau with trespass, assault, and battery. In response to Chouteau's brutality, the trial judge ordered Chouteau to bring the Scypion women to court for his inspection, directed Chouteau to allow the women conferences with their attorneys, and ordered him to post a bond to insure Chouteau's compliance with the court's orders.

Chouteau hired Luke E. Lawless and Horatio Cozens. When Cozens was killed, Chouteau hired Henry S. Geyer, a proslavery Whig who was one of the lawyers who argued against Dred Scott in the 1858 U.S. Supreme Court. Eventually, Tayon and Chouteau prevailed in the jury trial. The supreme court was divided equally in its decision of appeal, and so the circuit court verdict stood.

Never ones to give up, the Scypion women and their lawyers, five years after the jury trial, asked the Missouri Supreme Court to review the 1828 jury verdict and decision. By this time, the supreme court consisted of Isaac McGirk, his brother Matthias McGirk, and Robert Walsh. Their 1834 decision held that the previous trial had been invalid because the jury had been improperly instructed.

The case was transferred to Jefferson County, but since the county did not have a courthouse, the case was moved to Herculaneum. The parties agreed that they would try one of the cases, and the verdict in this one case would apply to all of them. The evidence consisted mostly of depositions, and the trial judge, Judge William Scott, gave instructions directed by the supreme court. On November 8, 1836, thirty-one years after its original filing, the case went to the jury, and the twelve-man jury ruled unanimously in favor of the Scypion family. Chouteau's lawyer appealed to the supreme court of Missouri, which upheld the circuit court. Chouteau then sought to appeal to the U.S. Supreme Court, which ruled that it did not have jurisdiction to hear the case *Chouteau v. Marguerite*, 37 U.S. 507 (1838).

Thirty-three years after the original suit filing, the Scypion family was declared free. From 1805 to 1838, when the Dred Scott case was filed, some 137 freedom suits had been filed. This was the first. After the Scott decision, freedom suits continued to be filed until 1860. After the Emancipation Proclamation and the passage of the Thirteenth Amendment, there was no longer any need for the freedom suits.

A question of "what might have been" is whether anyone would have tried to apply the Scypion theory to mulattos. The Scypions won their freedom because they were half Indian, even though they were half black. What might have happened if mulattos sued because they were half white? There is no found record of this issue having been tried.

Billy (William) Tarleton

The first freedom suit after the Louisiana Purchase was in 1814 when Billy Tarleton sued Jacob Horine. Horine claimed that he bought Billy from Squire Brooke of Jefferson County, Kentucky, and transcribed a copy of the bill of sale in an affidavit. Billy denied the bill of sale ever existed. A note from Horine asked for continuance to allow his brother to arrive with proof of ownership from Brooke. Billy sued for trespass, assault and battery, and false imprisonment and sought damages in the amount of one thousand dollars.

We know the case went to trial on October 25, 1814, because of the subpoenas issued to Joseph Kerr and John Bell. But the available records do not indicate whether Billy won or lost.

Billy was represented by David Barton, and Horine was represented by a lawyer with the last name of Carr.

THE ASPASIA SUITS

IT SEEMS THAT THERE WERE A FEW SEPARATE SUITS FILED BY SLAVES NAMED Aspasia, presumably a relatively common name. At least a couple seem to be against the Catholic bishop of St. Louis, Joseph Rosati.

Simpson v. Strother

NOT ALL OF THE SUITS INVOLVING ONE OR MORE ASPASIA INVOLVED A SUIT for freedom. In 1828, St. Louis Sheriff Robert Simpson sued George Strother for failing to pay the bond on which Strother was principal. The bond was for hiring Aspasia during her suit against Francois Chouteau. Simpson claimed Strother owed $500 for bond and $47.65 for the term of court during which she was hired out. Strother claimed Aspasia had been awarded her freedom and had written him clear of any charges. This is an example of pleading in the alternative, which is clearly allowed now, and was seemingly allowed 180 years ago as well, he also claimed to have already paid the sum for the term of hire. Isaac McGirk represented the sheriff, while Arthur Magenis represented Mr. Strother.

Aspasia v. Hardage Lane

IN 1837, FERDINAND RISQUE AND GUSTAVUS BIRD REPRESENTED THIS thirty-two-year-old daughter of Judy, who was called Old Judy. Henry Geyer, Thomas Hudson, and Wilson Primm represented Lane, an example of the willingness of Henry Geyer to represent either side in the freedom suits. Aspasia claimed to have been born in Vincennes, Indiana, and possessed a bill of sale in Spanish. The document cited decisions in Missouri in the freedom cases. She was unsuccessful in her suit.

The Bishop Rosati Suits

Many might assume that the leaders of the Catholic Church would have been supporters of the abolition of slavery. Quite to the contrary, slave ownership by the Catholic hierarchy was fairly common. Unfortunately, during this period of American history, some of the freedom suits involved the Catholic hierarchy. Bishop Joseph Rosati owned several slaves. Even at his death, his slave William is listed and the income from renting him out during the probate of Rosati's estate.[54] The slaves who sued for their freedom were not listed in Bishop Rosati's estate. Whether they died or were sold is not known.

It is also of interest, but no one seems to have an easy answer, that the bishop was the owner of significant land in Illinois, although he was the bishop of the St. Louis diocese, which did not include any Illinois land.

Aspasia v. Joseph Rosati

In 1837, the first of a few suits involving the Catholic hierarchy, was filed by Aspasia against Joseph Rosati, then the bishop of the St. Louis diocese. Ferdinand W. Risque, presumably not a Catholic willing to risk excommunication, represented Aspasia (also known as Aspisa). Aspasia claimed that her mother, Judy, had been held as a slave in Vincennes, Indiana, and Kaskaskia, Illinois, in the Northwest Territory, and was therefore freed. Aspasia's suit, based on her mother's suit for freedom, mentioned the Ordinance of 1787; Rosati's defense was that he rented her out. The court file is absent as to who won, but the indications are that the Catholic bishop got to keep his slave.

Significant is the fact that Luke Lawless was the trial judge.

Charles v. Rosati and Verhagen

IN 1840, THE SECOND SUIT AGAINST BISHOP ROSATI WAS FILED BY CHARLES. Peter Verhagen, a Belgian/Flemish Jesuit missionary, joined as a co-defendant. Charles claimed that he had been sent by his owner, Bishop Rosati, to Illinois to repair a "nunnery" in Cahokia for about ten or twelve days. The court seemingly concluded that this was not enough to meet the criteria for freedom, and Charles lost the suit.

Charles was represented by Trusten Polk and C. C. Carrol, while Bishop Rosati was represented by Wilson Primm.

JACK AND ARCH

JACK AND ARCH V. BARNABAS HARRIS LOOKS LIKE THE FIRST SUIT IN WHICH Joshua Barton represented a plaintiff. As good a lawyer as was Barton, he lost this one.

In 1819, Jack, who may have been joined in the suit by another slave called Arch, sued Barnabas Harris, claiming that they were originally owned by Eusebius Hubbard and Barnabas Harris of St. Ferdinand. Jack's suit included a copy of a deed of emancipation by Hubbard upon his death. The court record indicates a lot of documentary evidence, including:

- A bill of sale dated five days before Hubbard's death selling plaintiff and slave Arch to Barnabas Harris;

- Defendant became Frederick Hyatt, after Harris's death; Hyatt was the administrator to Harris's estate;

- A copy of a marriage contract between Elisabeth Bond and Eusebius Hubbard, which mentioned slaves Lucy, Milly, Hannah, Charlotte, Judy, Barn, Arch, Matt, Tye, and Jack;

- Eusebius's son George and son-in-law John Proctor listed on a bill of sale;

- A contract giving possession of Jack and Arch to John Proctor and George Hubbard upon Eusebius's death.

Apparently even in 1819 Missouri, the plaintiffs were allowed to plead in the alternative, since Jack claimed his previous owner, Eusebius Hubbard, emancipated him upon Hubbard's death. Jack was claimed as a slave by Harris. The court file included a document from the judge discussing the legality of slaves being entitled to a trial by jury. The trial judge, in his instructions, talked about the importance of the Magna

Carta and the Seventh Amendment to the U.S. Constitution (the right to a trial by jury). The slaves—Lucy, Milly, Hannah, Charlotte, Judy, Barn, Arch, Matt, Tye, and Jack—were all discussed by the judge. The final evidence included a contract giving possession of Jack and Arch to John Proctor and George Hubbard upon Eusebius's death. The judge ruled in favor of the defendant.

THE WINNY SUITS

THE MOST SIGNIFICANT OF THE WINNY SUITS WAS *WINNY V. WHITESIDES*. But before the Whitesides case reached the Missouri Supreme Court, there were other suits filed by various Winnys, which were of some significance. So it would be helpful to spend a few moments with the other suits, which did not go through the Missouri Supreme Court.[56] The major difference was that *Winny v. Whitesides* involved so many slaves and a huge financial loss to Whitesides.

Winny v. Samuel Donner

IN 1820, WINNY, WHO WAS ALSO CALLED LAC, SUED SAMUEL DONNER, claiming that Donner had seized, held, and forced her to do menial work without good cause. Winny's lawyer was James Beckhan, while Donner was represented by Matthias McGirk. Winny claimed that she had been the property of Jenning Beckwith, and Beckwith had sold her to Donner in 1817 for $300 with the indenture that she was to be freed at such time as she paid Donner $350. The judgment was entered in Winny's favor in the April term 1821 circuit court by N. B. Thiker. The judge's handwritten judgment set out his instructions to the jury that Donner's acceptance of $350 from Winny, which was alone sufficient evidence, would be sufficient for the jury to prove Winny's case. Donner's lawyer had argued, and asked the judge to instruct the jury, that the indenture was invalid because it was only subscribed to by one person and that it was never recorded, thus not binding on Donner. Judge Thiker refused to give the defense's jury instruction, and instead gave the plaintiff's re-quested instruction.

Even in this early stage of Missouri jury instructions, the judges tended to do "justice." In this case, Donner was not going to be able to keep Winny and her money.

Winny v. Rose

IN *WINNY V. ROSE*, WINNY—WHO HAD TWO CHILDREN, ELIZABETH, AGE four, and Bob, age two—claimed she was entitled to her freedom because of her sixteen-year residence in the Illinois Territory. Rose moved Winny to Missouri two years before this suit was filed in 1821 and Winny was his "indentured servant," according to the law of the Territory of Indiana. Rose "indentured" Winny for years of service, as recorded by the clerk of Common Pleas in Knox County, Indiana, to a Robert Buntin. Buntin was not identified further. The record reflects that Winny lost this suit. In this suit, Winny was represented by Rufus Pettibone, while Rose was represented by Joshua Barton, so we see the freedom suit giants squaring off early.

Winny v. John and Phoebe Whitesides

WINNY V. JOHN AND PHOEBE WHITESIDES WAS FILED IN 1819 AND WAS eventually tried in February 1822. It was a truly significant suit, for the principal reason that Winny won and the Missouri Territorial Supreme Court upheld the trial court's decision. The Missouri Supreme Court established an unquestionable precedent in these suits that was followed in the freedom suits until the Whig judges replaced the Democrats.

Phoebe Pruitt was originally from North Carolina. She and her husband, John Whitesides, brought Winny with them from North Carolina through the Illinois Territory to Missouri in 1798–99. Winny was born around 1783. We don't know what caused the Whitesides to leave North Carolina or to come to Missouri. By the time Winny filed her suit in 1819, she had eight children, all of whom filed separate suits based on the fact that Winny was free, and so should they: *Lydia v. John Butler* (Lydia freed); *Nancy v. Isaac Voteau*; *Jenny v. Robert Musick*; *Jerry v. Charles Hatton*; *Daniel v. John Whitesides*; *Hannah v. Phoebe Whitesides*; *Malinda v. Phoebe Whitesides*; and *Louis or Lewis v. John and Phoebe Whitesides*.

John Whitesides died in 1814, before Winny filed her suit. On his death, all of the slaves became the property of Phoebe, so the defendant was actually Phoebe Pruitt Whitesides. Later reference to Mr. Whitesides was to a Thomas Whitesides, Phoebe's son. The mere fact that it took so many separate suits to gain their freedom shows how persistent the Whitesides and Rufus Pettibone were. By the time this batch of litigation was over, the Whitesides and Rufus most likely felt pretty negatively about Barton and Geyer.

The confusion is further exacerbated by the fact that Rufus Pettibone and Josiah Spalding represented Milly in *Milly v. Rose*, while Rose was represented by Joshua Barton and Henry Geyer, but in *Milly v. Whitesides*, Joshua Barton and Henry Geyer represented Milly and all of the children in their suits while Rufus Pettibone and Josiah Spalding represented the defendants in *Milly v. Whitesides* and in Milly's children's suits.

As another example of how confused the litigation and claims became, in Winny's suit against Pettibone, she claimed that she was originally owned by Rufus Pettibone, who purchased or obtained her from Thomas Whitset and Owen Wingfield. John Whitset (alias John Whitesides), his wife, Phoebe, and son, Thomas, possessed Winny as a slave, and moved (circa 1792) from Kentucky to the Territory of the United States North West of the River Ohio, at or near a place then known as New Design or Whitesides' Station. Winny contends that she was held in slavery in violation of the laws of the Territory of the United States North West of the River Ohio. Around 1796, John, Phoebe, and Thomas Whitesides moved to Upper Louisiana in the neighborhood of St. Louis and brought Winny with them in slavery, against her consent. Upon the death of John Whitesides, Winny remained enslaved to Phoebe and Thomas Whitesides until about 1817 or 1818, when she was purchased by Rufus Pettibone, who refused to liberate her.

Another part of this complicated family feud was that Phoebe's daughters were claiming that she had given Winny and her family to them, and they had emancipated Winny. This claim never resolved the case, and the Missouri Supreme Court may have been looking for a case to establish the "once free, always free" rule, and so ignored the easy way out.

There appear to have been at least six separate suits against Matthias Rose, Ephraim Musick, Charles Hatton, Owen Wingfield, Isaac Butler, Rufus Pettibone, and Phoebe Whitesides. While there seems to be some confusion as to which defendants were actually involved in Winny's suits, this is a result of the legal "games" that Rufus Pettibone and Phoebe Whitesides were playing. At various stages of the litigation, Pettibone and Whitesides would sell or transfer the family members to each other and others in order to defeat the pending litigation. Ultimately, Joshua Barton and Henry Geyer overcame the Pettibone/Whitesides tricks by filing multiple suits against multiple defendants, and with a little bit of judicial pressure forced Pettibone and Whitesides to agree to try one lawsuit, the results of which would apply to all. Winny's original lawyer was James Beckwith. In each of the other cases Joshua Barton and Henry Geyer represented the plaintiffs, and Rufus Pettibone and Josiah Spalding represented the losing defendants.

Ultimately the lawyers agreed, I suspect with the "encouragement" of the judge, that they would actually go to trial on one of the suits, and the results of that one case would apply to all of the cases. The "consolidated" cases were *Winny v. Pettibone, Malinda v. Pettibone, Harry v. Pettibone, Larinda v. Pettibone, Winny v Musick, et al.,* and *Mennetta v. Musick, et al.*

Winny was allowed to sue as a poor person, and as a condition of the waiver of costs, the court ordered that neither Winny nor any of her children be removed from the county, *and* that the sheriff hire them out to whomever he wanted for the best price he could get, *and* he should keep the "rental" until the court decided what to do with it. We never did find out what happened to the rental the sheriff collected.

In *Winny v. Whitesides*, the jury found in favor of Winny and her children. Whitesides appealed to the newly formed Missouri Supreme Court. Judges Matthias McGirk and George Tompkins maintained that the laws of Illinois applied as to whether taking a slave into a free state freed the slave. This was the basis, the precedent, and for some twenty years it controlled the outcome of the freedom suits.

The irony of the Missouri decision was that the Missouri court held that the Illinois law, which prohibited slavery, was the basis for declaring that a slave, who had been moved to Illinois, for as short a time as one month, allowed the Illinois law to apply, and bringing the slave into Missouri freed the slave. Illinois courts, whose law applied, would not, however, provide for the freeing of the slave who had been brought into Illinois. Missouri would free the slave based on Illinois law, but Illinois would not free the slave applying Illinois law.[57]

A question never posed was whether a slave taken into Illinois and never brought back to Missouri would ever have been freed.

THE WALKER SUITS

In 1826, the state of Missouri sued John K. Walker (jailor of St. Louis), Pierre Chouteau, and Bernard Pratt; Alexis Amelin sued the defendants to compel a habeas corpus. Amelin was an agent for Alexander Scott, captain of the steamboat *General Brown*. The four slaves suing for freedom were Catherine, Julia, Helen, and Joseph.

Then in 1834, James Henry sued William Walker. James was the mulatto son of Rachel, from *Rachel v. Walker*. James was born at Prairie du Chien, Michigan Territory (now Wisconsin), while owned by T. B. W. Stockton. He brought suit by his next friend, Josiah Spalding.

In 1834, Rachel, a woman of color, sued William Walker. This suit is described in the companion case, *Rachel v. Stockton*. The Stockton case is another of the "games" the owners were playing, by transferring the people trying to get free, and was the precursor of *Winny v. Whitesides*, which established the "once free, always free" rule in Missouri. This is one of the cases that was cited only by its location, which was specifically overruled in Dred Scott's Missouri Supreme Court decision.

In 1835, Mary Farnham sued Samuel D. Walker. Mary, who was twenty-one or twenty-two years old, was born in Ste. Genevieve, Missouri, in the family of John B. Bussier. Mary was brought to St. Louis and sold to Russell Farnham, who moved to Lower Rapids on the Mississippi River at Fort Edwards. Farnham came to St. Louis and died in October 1832.

In 1835, Mary Ann Steel sued William Walker, as a poor person, by her next friend G. A. Bird; Mary Ann was sixteen at the time she filed her suit. She claimed that she had been the slave of Catherine Steel of Kentucky, and that Catherine had emancipated Mary Ann in 1821 by her last will. Catherine had originally acquired Mary Ann in the will of James Steel. Judge Lawless, in June 1835, entered an order prohibiting Mary Ann from being taken from the court's jurisdiction, reflecting a practice by some of these defendants of shipping the slaves out of the territory, so the court could not rule on the slave's petition for freedom. As a matter of fact, in at least fourteen cases, the plaintiffs lost their suit because they were shipped out of the court's jurisdiction and did not show up for the trial.

As happened in several of these freedom suits, the family of the "owners" were split on whether to try to protect the freedom of the plaintiffs. In this case, the heirs of James Steel contested the will, but the will was upheld and Mary Ann went free.

Rachel v. Stockton

ANOTHER EXAMPLE OF THE KIND OF CASE WHERE THE MEMBERS OF THE family of the "owner" were split on who should win, or whether the plaintiff should have been freed, arose in 1834 when "Rachel, a mulatto woman," sued William Walker for her freedom.[58] Rachel had been purchased in St. Louis for an army officer, Thomas B. W. Stockton, stationed at Fort Snelling (at the time, Wisconsin Territory, where Dred Scott was taken, also by an army officer) in 1830.[59] Stockton took Rachel to Washington, D.C., in 1832, then to Fort Crawford, Michigan, for two years, where her son James Henry was born.[60] In 1834 Rachel found herself and James Henry sold and resold, finally "to one William Walker," who was a slave trader. Rachel claimed that Walker was about to take her and her child down the Mississippi River probably to New Orleans for sale. In this case, the court assigned Josiah Spalding as counsel to represent Rachel, and Hamilton Gamble represented Stockton. This case is of interest because we have Spalding, Gamble, Luke Lawless, and McGirk all involved. It was a little like an all-star game with the big hitters showing their stuff.

According to Stockton's deposition, "[D]uring all the time I owned her and her child, and I was an officer of the United States army, stationed at those different posts by order of the proper authority. Rachel was never employed otherwise than as my private servant and in immediate attendance upon my family."[61] Lawless instructed the St. Louis jury that such employment was a necessary "incident" to Stockton's military duties.

The court thereupon decided the law governing the case to be, that if said Stockton was an officer of the army of the United States while he held the plaintiff in slavery stationed in Fort Snelling and Fort Crawford by the proper authority, and if he employed the plaintiff during that time only in personal attendance on himself and family, that such residence of the plaintiff at those places as has been proved does not entitle her to her freedom.

Lawless's instructions allowed the St. Louis jury to interpret the law that sanctioned the keeping of a slave "as my private servant and in immediate attendance on my family" as a necessity justifying an exception to the ban on slavery. Justice Matthias McGirk of the Missouri Supreme Court recognized the stratagem of arguing to the jury "to induce the belief of the fact that the service she performed was necessary or perhaps to establish the fact that the officer has a right to a family servant."[62] He rejected both assumptions as a legal definition of "necessary"; keeping a slave was only a "convenience," not a necessity, and "no law nor public authority required him [Stockton] to keep the person as a slave nor as a servant."[63]

Losing in the circuit court, Rachel appealed to the state supreme court, where she won. In 1836 the Missouri Supreme Court ruled in favor of Rachel, one of the decisions establishing "its tendency to enforce the laws of the neighboring free states," that a slaveholder forfeited rights to a slave by taking it into free territory. By the time the case reached the supreme court, it involved only Rachel; she had to file a separate suit to free her son James Henry. The court continued with the precedent of *Winny v. Whitesides* (1824), in which the state supreme court held that a slave was free after being held in a free state, and "once free, always free." This ruling was cited in 1856 in the famous *Dred Scott v. Sandford* case before the Supreme Court of the United States.

In keeping with *Winny v. Whitesides*, Justice Matthias McGirk of the Missouri Supreme Court said that Stockton had "willfully procured a slave and held her, unlawfully, in free territories, an act punishable by forfeiture of the slave, as decreed by territorial law." Her success in this case supported her second case to free her son. (Perhaps her attorneys recommended that the cases be separated after she filed her initial petition.) She also gained freedom for her son; as he was born to a woman considered at that time legally free because of her extended residency in a free state. He was also free according to the principle of *partus*.

Mary Farnum v. Samuel Walker

In 1835, Mary Farnum sued Samuel Walker, alleging that Mary, then twenty-one or twenty-two years old, was born in Ste. Genevieve, Missouri, in the family of John B. Bussier; she was brought to St. Louis, sold to Russell Farnham who moved to Lower Rapids on the Mississippi River at Fort Edwards; Farnham came to St. Louis and died in October 1832.

Berry v. Mitchell

Polly Berry was known by a couple other names, Polly Crockett and Polly Wash. The name's Berry, Crockett, and Wash were the names of her "owners." She was born free around 1818 and died sometime between 1870 and 1880. She sued on October 3, 1839, a suit based on having been held in the free state of Illinois for a time. She won in 1843. What is known of her personal life comes to us through her daughter's memoir, *From the Darkness Cometh the Light, or, Struggles for Freedom*, published in 1891 under her married name of Lucy Delaney. Delaney's memoir suggests that Polly's attorneys recommended she file separate suits for her and her daughter to prevent the jury from worrying about taking too much property from one slaveholder. Delaney dedicated the book to the Grand Army of the Republic, which had secured the freedom of slaves throughout the South in its victory in the American Civil

War. She also described her adult life and participation in religious and civic organizations.

Polly testified that she was held as a child slave in Wayne County, Kentucky by Joseph Crockett. When she was about fourteen, Crockett took her to Illinois, where they stayed for several weeks. Crockett hired out Polly for domestic servant tasks, and she was then known as Polly Crockett, after her "master." Crockett took her up the Missouri River for about five years. Polly was then sold to a Major Taylor Berry in St. Louis, Missouri, hence the name Berry. She married one of his slaves, said to be a mulatto, and they had two daughters, Nancy and Lucy Ann Berry.

Following the major's death, his widow Franny Berry, married a few years later, Robert Wash, one of three Missouri Supreme Court justices. Fanny Wash died a few years after the wedding. Contrary to the provisions of Major Berry's will to free the slaves, Fanny's widower Robert Wash sold Polly's husband "down the river" to a plantation in the Deep South. However, the best efforts of their "masters" could not curtail Polly and her daughters. Eventually, all of them successfully escaped.

Polly Berry prepared her daughters to escape their respective masters. For instance, when Nancy Berry was accompanying Mary Berry Coxe and her husband on their honeymoon to Niagara Falls, she fled successfully across the river by ferry to Canada, where she remained with a friend of her mother's. Nancy moved to Toronto, where she married and had her own family.

Martha Berry Mitchell, another of the married daughters of the late Major Berry, claimed Lucy Ann Berry as a domestic servant. Angered over the girl's lack of ability to do laundry, Mitchell got into a physical confrontation with her, and Martha and her husband David D. Mitchell decided to sell the young slave down the river. (Mitchell was the U.S. Regional Superintendent for Indian Affairs.) Before being shipped away, Lucy Ann escaped to the house of a friend of her mother.

Polly Berry escaped shortly after in 1839, from Mary Berry Coxe when she had been sold to Joseph M. Magehan, a lumberman. She traveled as far as Chicago before being apprehended by slave catchers. They returned her to St. Louis and her master Magehan. She resolved to protect her daughter Lucy Ann, who was only twelve years old.

Once back in St. Louis, Polly sued (*Polly Wash v. Joseph M. Magehan*). Her lawyer was Harris Sprout. But it was not until 1843 that she successfully proved her case in court. While the case was pending, as was the practice by this time, Polly was hired out as a laundress to earn money against her upkeep.

In 1842 Polly sued for Lucy Ann Berry's freedom in a case argued by Edward Bates against David D. Mitchell as a "next friend" of her daughter. Lucy Ann was fourteen years old. Because Wash's case had not yet been tried, she was still considered a slave and had no individual legal standing. According to the doctrine of *partus*, since Lucy Ann was born to a woman considered free in Illinois, she should also be free. Lucy was remanded to jail, where she stayed for seventeen months rather than being hired out, as was customary. Polly's attorneys were thus successful in ensuring that Lucy Ann Berry was kept in St. Louis.

Lucy's case was not heard until February 1844. Her attorneys argued that Lucy Berry's freedom was based on her birth to a woman who had been proven to be free based on having been held in Illinois. Francis B. Murdoch prepared the case for Lucy and her trial lawyer, Edward Bates. Murdoch handled a lot of the "freedom suits" in St. Louis. Bates was able to convince the jury that since Polly should be free, Lucy Ann should be free as well.

Aftermath

POLLY AND LUCY LIVED TOGETHER FOR THE REST OF POLLY'S LIFE AT FIRST as seamstresses. Polly managed to visit her daughter Nancy and grandchildren in Toronto in 1845. Nancy offered to settle Lucy there, but Polly chose to return Lucy Ann to her St. Louis roots. She died without seeing her husband again.[64]

The Burd Suits

William Burd was defending six suits over a four-year period. The first of five were by the William Stubbs family. These were all based on the allegation that William Stubbs was born to free parents in Virginia. Burd was originally from Campbell County, Virginia. Hamilton Gamble represented Burd while George Strother represented the Stubbs family. The Stubbs were set free.

The last suit Burd defended was in 1841, a suit by Louis Scott, who claimed that Burd had brought Scott to St. Clair County, Illinois, to repair "copper kettles or stills" that Burd purchased. Scott lost in the circuit court and the case was appealed to the Missouri Supreme Court. This time around, Jeremiah Langton represented Scott, and by this time Hamilton Gamble was on the Missouri Supreme Court, so Joshua Spalding represented Burd. Spalding did a more effective job for his client than did Gamble in the earlier suits. Scott lost his case.

THE CHOUTEAU SUITS

IN ADDITION TO THE PLETHORA OF SUITS GENERATED BY THE WHITESIDES family, the Chouteaus were involved in a significant number of other freedom suits. Some they won, and some they lost.

Marie v. Auguste Chouteau

THE FIRST FREEDOM SUIT INVOLVING THE CHOUTEAUS WAS IN 1821, IN *MARIE v. Auguste Chouteau*. Henry Geyer represented Marie, while Edward Bates represented the Chouteaus. This is illustrative of these two lawyers squaring off against each other in the courtroom. Marie was under the age of twenty-one and sued through her next friend and mother, Marguerite. Marie claimed that her former owner, Nicholas Beugenoux, took her to St. Clair County, Territory of Illinois, and there he sold her to Auguste, who brought her back when he returned to St. Louis. According to the transcript of the court's minute entries in the case, Geyer won, one of several of his victories during the 1821 salvo of freedom suits. His string of wins seemed to concentrate on suing the Whitesides and the Chouteaus.

Aspasia v. Francois Chouteau and Pierre Menard

IN 1828, ASPASIA, ALSO CALLED ASPASIE, CLAIMING TO HAVE BEEN BORN IN Kaskaskia, Illinois, to a Negro mother in 1806, was held in slavery by Baptiste Jeandreau. Jeandreau sold Aspasia to Colonel Pierre Menard in 1827, who then gave her to Francois Chouteau and his wife, who was Pierre's daughter. Included in the court papers was an affidavit indicating that the defendants, who lived in St. Louis, were about to move her down the river by the steamboat *America*.

Aspasia was represented by Isaac McGuire and John Bent, and

Chouteau and Menard were represented by Josiah Spalding and Beverly Allen. This Aspasia won her freedom.

Pierre v. Gabriel Chouteau

IN 1842, PIERRE SUED CHOUTEAU, CLAIMING THAT HIS MOTHER, ROSE, WAS brought from Montreal to Illinois by John Stork. Pierre claimed that he was sold with his two children to Andrew Todd, then to Pierre Didier of St. Louis, who ultimately sold them to Auguste Chouteau. Pierre's claim was based on the notion that his mother was born free in a "British Province in which slavery is not tolerated." Pierre was represented by Wilson Primm, Francis B. Murdoch, and George Taylor. Chouteau was again represented by Joshua Spalding. Pierre won, and the case was appealed to the supreme court.

Feelings against slavery by this time had become strong among much of the community, to the extent that one of the questions that was proposed to be asked of the jurors was whether any of them felt conscience bound to find for the plaintiff not withstanding that the law "might hold him in slavery." The judge refused to allow the question to be asked. This issue was one of the questions on appeal. Judge William Scott, writing for the court, reversed the jury verdict for Pierre, commenting on the circuit judge's refusal to allow the jurors to be asked whether they would vote to free Pierre regardless of what the law might be. This was not the only reason for reversing Pierre's verdict, causing the case to be remanded to the circuit court. There was a question as to when slavery was abolished and prohibited in Canada, and whether Pierre's mother was free. The freedom suit files do not indicate the results of the retrial, but given the supreme court's decision, it seems that it might have been a hard road for Pierre on the retrial.[65]

Mary Charlotte v. Pierre Chouteau

IN ANOTHER 1843 SUIT AGAINST PIERRE CHOUTEAU, MARY CHARLOTTE SUED for herself, her husband, and four children, Antoine, Auguste, Victorine, and Euphrasia. The suit claimed she was born in Montreal, Canada, in 1791. She was then taken by an Indian trader named John Stock to his trading post in Ohio where he kept her as his slave until he died in 1793. Eventually, she was sold to Auguste Chouteau. When Auguste died, she was inherited by Pierre Chouteau. Mary lost in the circuit court, principally because the circuit judge would not allow her to put into evidence the records showing that her mother was born free in Canada. Her case was appealed to the supreme court, and in 1855, Judge George Tompkins wrote the opinion that her evidence regarding her mother's Canadian parentage should not have been excluded, and remanded the case for retrial, with the order to admit her evidence as to her mother's Canadian birth.[66]

We could not find within the freedom suit records the result of the retrial.

Theotiste v. Pierre Chouteau

THEOTISTE, A.K.A. CATICHE, WAS BORN IN PRAIRIE DU ROCHER, ILLINOIS, IN 1782, owned by the Bourbeau family. She was later sold to Manuel Lisa. After Lisa's death, the plaintiff was sold at public sale to the defendant. Chouteau won this one.

Francois La Grange Alias Isidore v. Chouteau

THIS CASE'S RECORDS WERE NOT RETRIEVED AS PART OF THE FREEDOM SUITS project but were recorded in the supreme court's records.[67] The plaintiff, also called Isidore, or Isadore, claimed he was born in St. Louis as a slave of Pascal Cerre. Chouteau wanted to buy him from Cerre, but Cerre sold him to Pierre Menard of Kaskaskia, Illinois, because Cerre wanted to sell Isidore to someone outside St. Louis. Menard, an Illinois resident living in Kansas, took Isidore to Ste. Genevieve and then to Washington County to work in the mines, and then to Kaskaskia where Isidore worked on a keelboat and went down the river to New Orleans. After some other river work, Isidore was returned to St. Louis and sold to Chouteau. The jury returned a verdict for Chouteau, and in the bill of exceptions was a summary of the testimony of Menard. Menard claimed he had not purchased the plaintiff for himself from Cerre because he lived in Illinois, but he had purchased him for Chouteau, a resident of St. Louis.

To get around Cerre's desire to sell Isidore to someone outside Missouri, the supreme court took up the issue of the "scheme" of Menard and Chouteau to circumvent the desire of Cerre to sell the slave so he would be taken out of Missouri and pointed out that the "scheme" of Menard and Chouteau was clearly contrary to the desire of Cerre. The facts were decided in the decision by Judge Robert Walsh that Isidore was taken to Ste. Genevieve, and then to Washington County, and then hired out to work the keelboats, but Isidore never accompanied his owner to a location outside the state of Missouri. Judge Walsh decided that Menard never bought Isidore with the intention of moving him to Menard's residence in Kaskaskia.

The supreme court did nothing to overturn the Winny case but did add what would seem to be a natural increment of the rule—that there had to be some contemporaneous residence of the slave and the owner in the free territory. Judge Walsh clearly set out the criteria for the kind of residence in a free state that would win the plaintiff his or her freedom.

The owner of a slave removing to Illinois and carrying his slave along with him to reside there permanently must intend to introduce 'involuntary servitude or slavery' against the express terms of the ordinance: but the owner of a slave who was merely passing through the country with him, or maybe a resident in Illinois and may choose to imploring him in Missouri in mining or as a sailor or boat hand upon the river or the high seas or vessels that occasionally lade or unlade to their cargoes at some port or place within the state, though we may not do much in extending the fundamental principles of civil and religious liberty, certainly does not think forward in grasping slavery upon the social system of the state.

The question remains what kind of result might have occurred if Cerre had sued to set aside Isidore's sale to Menard on the basis of Menard's fraudulent representation that he would take Isidore to Illinois as a part of his permanent residence. Since the question was never raised at the time, and since the laws have changed in the last 180 years, this question may be an interesting law school exercise, but we will never know.

The Menard Suits

With the exception of the Chouteau family, perhaps no other St. Louis family was so forceful in defending its ownership of slaves than the Menards.

The family members were sued some seventeen times. In 1826, John Merry, represented by Joseph Charless and Isaac McGirk, sued Louise Menard, who was represented by Luke Lawless and Edward Bates. The plaintiff, also called Jean Marie in depositions of witnesses, was around the age of thirty-five or thirty-six. John Merry claimed he was born a slave in Cahokia, Illinois, after the Ordinance of 1787. Pensino, also Peceneau and Piceneau, claimed the plaintiff and his parents as slaves and sold the plaintiff to his son Lewis Piceneau. There was a verbal contract between Lewis and plaintiff for purchasing his freedom for $450 to be paid in three years. The plaintiff claimed he paid Piceneau $200 and two horses for a total of $230 before the three-year period expired. Piceneau gave him freedom to work off the rest of the money. The plaintiff then moved to St. Louis, where he was seized on Piceneau's orders and taken by steamboat to New Orleans and sold to Andrew Shecksni, from whom he "absconded" and returned to Cahokia. John Merry was recaptured and brought to St. Louis, where he was repossessed by defendants. The court file depositions mentioned a steamboat *General Brown* on which the plaintiff was bound in irons. The first bill of exceptions stated plaintiff had a verbal contract to purchase not only himself but his wife and two children for $900. The supreme court justice granted a new trial in the circuit court and included a second bill of instructions and jury instructions. Ultimately, the plaintiff won his freedom in the retrial.

In 1827, Mary, represented by Isaac McGirk and John Bass, sued Francois Menard, who was represented by George Strother. The plaintiff claimed to be born in Kaskaskia, Illinois, and owned by Michel

Bivenue. After Bivenue's death, Mary was sold to Francois Menard and brought to St. Louis about three years prior to filing suit in custody of Andre Landreville. The plaintiff's petition included daughters Virginia, age seven, Victoire, age six, and Elisabeth, age three. The plaintiffs lost this round.

Then in 1829, Mary sued Francois Menard. This suit was joined by suits for Elizabeth, Virginia, and Victoire. By this time the slave owners were getting more sophisticated in thwarting suits. Slave owners used additional schemes to avoid losing the slaves, since, in this case, the sheriff's return indicated that Francois could not be found. In 1839, never quitting, the women again sued, this time represented by John Darby, listing all the activity on her suit since the original petition filed on July 31, 1827. When she was twenty-six or twenty-seven, at the time of the original filing, an original petition stated she was born in Kaskaskia, Illinois, into the family and ownership of Michel Bivenue. Upon Bivenue's death, she was sold to Francois Menard, who sent her to St. Louis to be hired out three years prior to her petition. She was hired out to Andre Landreville, whom she brought her original suit against along with Menard. Landreville denied ownership, and Menard stayed out of jurisdiction of the court, avoiding trial. As the suit continued, Menard evaded the trial until her previous attorneys, Isaac McGirk and John Bass, either died or "left the states." Her original suit abated for want of someone to present it. She and her eldest daughter, Virginia, age thirteen, had recently been seized by Sidney Brase and Daniel Busby, acting as agents of Menard, to prevent her from bringing a new suit. Menard continued to stay out of jurisdiction of the court, but Virginia prayed to allow suit for herself and her children, Virginia, Victoire, now age twelve, and Elizabeth, age eight.

Then in 1835, Mary Johnson, represented by James Mayfield and James Bowlin, sued Michael Menard, represented by Lewis Bogg. The plaintiff, about thirty-two years old, claimed to be born in Kaskaskia and owned by Michael Bivenue, deceased. Mary Johnson alleged Bivenue manumitted her with all his other slaves and servants in his will. The plaintiff had been living free for the past twelve months in St. Louis until claimed by the defendant as a slave.

This suit seems to have been coupled with the Agnis suit. The plaintiff, Agnis, about twenty-two years old, also claimed she was born in Kaskaskia, Illinois. Agnis's mother, an indentured servant or slave, believed that the plaintiff was never indentured or registered as an indentured servant. She left Illinois four years earlier and moved to St. Louis. A few days before filing the suit, the defendant, Menard, had claimed Agnis as his slave. The file indicates that the defendant was about to move Agnis out of the state, causing her to "lose all evidence of her freedom." The file also included a petition from the defendant for a change of venue and bond by Beverly Allen to guarantee Menard's appearance at a different venue.

Freedom Suit Summaries

The following pages list the summaries of all available Missouri freedom suits, including those featured earlier.

1806

Plaintiff:	Marie Scipion Descendants
Defendant:	Tayon, Joseph
Plaintiff's Attorney:	Isaac Danielle
Defendant's Attorney:	N/A
Verdict:	Freed

1814

Plaintiff:	Tarleton, Billy (William)
Defendant:	Horine, Jacob
Plaintiff's Attorney:	Barton, D.
Defendant's Attorney:	Carr
Verdict:	N/A
Notes:	

Plaintiff also known as Bill or Billy; township of Joachim, St. Louis County, Missouri Territory; defendant claimed bought plaintiff from Squire Brooke of Jefferson County, Kentucky; transcribed a copy of the bill of sale in affidavit; plaintiff denied said bill of sale ever existed; note from defendant asking for continuance to allow his brother to arrive with proof of ownership from Brooke.

1818

Plaintiff:	Jack
Defendant:	Harris, Barnabas
Plaintiff's Attorney:	Barton, Joshua; Gay, A.
Defendant's Attorney:	Carr
Verdict:	Not freed
Notes:	

Plaintiff originally owned by Eusebius Hubbard; township of St. Ferdinand; included copy of deed of emancipation by Hubbard upon his death; bill of sale dated five days before Hubbard's death selling plaintiff and slave Arch to Barnabas Harris; defendant became Frederick Hyatt, after Harris's death; Hyatt administrator to Harris's estate; copy of marriage contract between Elisabeth Bond and Eusebius Hubbard; mentioned slaves Lucy, Milly, Hannah, Charlotte, Judy, Barn, Arch, Matt, Tye, and Jack; Eusebius's son George and son-in-law John Proctor listed on bill of sale; contract giving possession of Jack and Arch to John Proctor and George Hubbard upon Eusebius's death.

1818

Plaintiff:	Arch
Defendant:	Harris, Barnabas
Plaintiff's Attorney:	N/A
Defendant's Attorney:	N/A
Verdict:	N/A
Notes:	

Plaintiff claimed previous owner, Eusebius Hubbard, emancipated plaintiff upon his death; claimed as slave by defendant; included document from Judge discussing the legality of slaves being entitled to trial by jury; mentioned Magna Carta and 7th amendment to Constitution; slaves Lucy, Milly, Hannah, Charlotte, Judy, Barn, Arch, Matt, Tye, and Jack; included contract giving possession of Jack and Arch to John Proctor and George Hubbard upon Eusebius's death; File same day as Jack, case #111.

1819

Plaintiff:	Milly
Defendant:	Mathias Rose
Plaintiff's Attorney:	Pettibone, Rufus

Defendant's Attorney:	Barton, Joshua
Verdict:	Not freed
Notes:	

Plaintiff and her two children, Elizabeth, age four, and Bob, age two; claimed entitled her freedom due to her sixteen year residence in Territory of Illinois; defendant removed to Missouri two years earlier; defendant claimed plaintiff as servant, according to law of Territory of Indiana; he indentured Milly for seventy years of service, as recorded by clerk of Common Pleas in Knox County, Indiana, Robert Buntin.

1820

Plaintiff:	Winny
Defendant:	Donner, Samuel
Plaintiff's Attorney:	Beckwith, James H.
Defendant's Attorney:	McGirk, M.
Verdict:	Freed
Notes:	

Plaintiff formerly owned by Jennings Beckwith; claimed Beckwith sold her to defendant for $300 on terms that she be indentured to Donner until she paid $350; upon paying that sum, she would be emancipated; plaintiff alleged she had paid Donner the amount required but was still enslaved; included notices of attachment; bill of exceptions included transcript of indenture agreement between Beckwith and Donner.

1821

Plaintiff:	Winny
Defendant:	Whitesides, a.k.a. Pruitt
Plaintiff's Attorney:	Barton, Joshua; Geyer, Henry S.
Defendant's Attorney:	Pettibone, Rufus; Spalding, Josiah
Verdict:	Freed
Notes:	

Plaintiff name also spelled Winne and Winney; claimed defendant, also called Pruitt and her husband John Whitesides carried her into the Territory of Indiana and held her there as a slave; defendant later moved her to Territory of Missouri; defendant claimed in request for continuance that Winny belonged to her children; petition included Winny's children Jerry, David, Jenny, Nancy, Lydia, Sarah, Hannah, Lewis, and Malinda.

1821

Plaintiff:	Sarah
Defendant:	Hatton, Mitchell
Plaintiff's Attorney:	Barton, Joshua; Geyer, Henry S.
Defendant's Attorney:	Pettibone, Rufus; Spalding, Josiah
Verdict:	Freed

Notes:

Plaintiff daughter of Winny; suit based on claim that Winny entitled to freedom for residence in Indiana Territory, "now Illinois"; defendant did not own Winny; plaintiff born after Winny's residence in free territory; included bill of exceptions; request to dismiss suit for lack of petition.

1821

Plaintiff:	Winny
Defendant:	Whitesides, Phoebe
Plaintiff's Attorney:	N/A
Defendant's Attorney:	N/A
Verdict:	N/A

Notes:

Plaintiff formerly owned by Jennings Beckwith; claimed Beckwith sold her to defendant for $300 on terms that she be indentured to Donner until she paid $350; upon paying that sum, she would be emancipated; plaintiff alleged she had paid Donner the amount required but was still enslaved; included notices of attachment; bill of exceptions included transcript of indenture agreement between Beckwith and Donner.

1821

Plaintiff:	Lydia
Defendant:	Butler, John
Plaintiff's Attorney:	Barton, Joshua; Geyer, Henry S.
Defendant's Attorney:	Pettibone, Rufus; Spalding, Josiah
Verdict:	Freed

Notes:

Plaintiff daughter of Winny; suit based on claim that Winny entitled to freedom for residence in Indiana Territory, "now Illinois"; defendant did not own Winny; plaintiff born after Winny's residence in free territory; included bill of exceptions.

1821

Plaintiff:	Nancy
Defendant:	Voteau, Isaac
Plaintiff's Attorney:	Barton, Joshua; Geyer, Henry S.
Defendant's Attorney:	Pettibone, Rufus; Spalding, Josiah
Verdict:	Freed
Notes:	

Plaintiff daughter of Winny; suit based on claim that Winny entitled to freedom for residence in Indiana Territory, "now Illinois"; defendant did not own Winny; affidavit from defendant asking for a continuance; claimed needed same witness Phoebe Pruitt requested in her suit against Winny; witness could verify Winny belonged to children of Phoebe and John Whitesides; included bill of exceptions.

1821

Plaintiff:	Jenny
Defendant:	Musick, Robert
Plaintiff's Attorney:	Barton, Joshua; Geyer, Henry S.
Defendant's Attorney:	Pettibone, Rufus; Spalding, Josiah
Verdict:	Freed
Notes:	

Plaintiff daughter of Winny; suit based on claim that Winny entitled to freedom for residence in Indiana Territory, "now Illinois"; defendant did not own Winny; affidavit from defendant asking for a continuance; needed same witness Phoebe Pruitt requested in her suit against Winny; included bill of exceptions.

1821

Plaintiff:	Jerry
Defendant:	Hatton, Charles
Plaintiff's Attorney:	Barton, Joshua; Geyer, Henry S.
Defendant's Attorney:	Pettibone, Rufus; Spalding, Josiah
Verdict:	Freed
Notes:	

Plaintiff son of Winny; suit based on claim that Winny entitled to freedom for residence in Indiana Territory, "now Illinois"; defendant did not own Winny; included bill of exceptions.

1821

Plaintiff:	Daniel
Defendant:	Whitesides, John
Plaintiff's Attorney:	Barton, Joshua; Geyer, Henry S.
Defendant's Attorney:	Pettibone, Rufus; Spalding, Josiah
Verdict:	Freed
Notes:	

Plaintiff son of Winny; suit based on claim that Winny entitled to freedom for residence in Indiana Territory, "now Illinois"; affidavit from defendant asking for a continuance; needed same witness Phoebe Pruitt requested in her suit against Winny; included bill of exceptions.

1821

Plaintiff:	Hannah
Defendant:	Whitesides, Phoebe
Plaintiff's Attorney:	Barton, Joshua; Geyer, Henry S.
Defendant's Attorney:	Pettibone, Rufus; Spalding, Josiah
Verdict:	Freed
Notes:	

Plaintiff daughter of Winny; suit based on claim that Winny entitled to freedom from residence in Indiana Territory, "now Illinois"; included bill of exceptions; defendant also known as Pruitt.

1821

Plaintiff:	Malinda
Defendant:	Whitesides, Phoebe
Plaintiff's Attorney:	Barton, Joshua; Geyer, Henry S.
Defendant's Attorney:	Pettibone, Rufus; Spalding, Josiah
Verdict:	Freed
Notes:	

Plaintiff daughter of Winny; suit based on claim that Winny entitled to freedom from residence in Indiana Territory, "now Illinois"; included bill of exceptions; defendant also known as Pruitt.

1821

Plaintiff:	Louis/Lewis
Defendant:	Whitesides, John and Phoebe
Plaintiff's Attorney:	Barton, Joshua; Geyer, Henry S.
Defendant's Attorney:	Pettibone, Rufus; Spalding, Josiah
Verdict:	Freed
Notes:	

Plaintiff son of Winny; suit based on claim that Winny entitled to freedom from residence in Indiana Territory, "now Illinois"; included bill of exceptions; defendant also known as Pruitt.

1821

Plaintiff:	Marie
Defendant:	Chouteau, Auguste
Plaintiff's Attorney:	Geyer, Henry S.
Defendant's Attorney:	Bates, [Edward R.]; Barton, Joshua
Verdict:	Freed
Notes:	

Plaintiff under the age of twenty-one; sued through next friend and mother Marguerite; claimed former owner Nicholas Beugenoux took her to St. Clair County, Territory of Illinois; sold to defendant upon returning to St. Louis; included transcript of minutes from the case.

1821

Plaintiff:	Chevalier, Helene
Defendant:	Rector, William, and John Little
Plaintiff's Attorney:	N/A
Defendant's Attorney:	N/A
Verdict:	Freed

1821

Plaintiff:	Chevalier, Ellen (Deceased)
Defendant:	Chouteau, Pierre
Plaintiff's Attorney:	N/A
Defendant's Attorney:	N/A
Verdict:	Freed

1821

Plaintiff:	Labon
Defendant:	Price, Risdon H.
Plaintiff's Attorney:	McGirk, Matthias.; Barton, Joshua
Defendant's Attorney:	Benton
Verdict:	Freed
Notes:	

Plaintiff also called Labourne; husband of Tempe; claimed brought from Kentucky to Territory of Illinois by owner William Clark; sold as a slave to Simon Vanorsdale; sold to defendant; claimed entitled freedom due to residence in free territory; included copy of Laban's record from the record of indentured servants of St. Clair County, Illinois; transcript of minutes and proceedings of the suit included a list of jurors; bill of exceptions.

1821

Plaintiff:	Tempe
Defendant:	Price, Risdon H.
Plaintiff's Attorney:	McGirk, Matthias; Barton, Joshua
Defendant's Attorney:	Benton
Verdict:	Freed
Notes:	

Plaintiff name also spelled Tempy; claimed she, along with her husband Laban, entered into a term indenture with Simon Vanosdol (also Vanorsdale); St. Clair County, Illinois; both agreed to finish indenture with defendant; included affidavits from Laban and Tempe complaining Tempe was being punished by defendant for bringing suit; deposition from Judge William Biggs, claiming at time of transfer, Tempe had ten or eleven years left of servitude.

1821

Plaintiff:	Pelagie
Defendant:	Valois, Francois
Plaintiff's Attorney:	Peck, James H.
Defendant's Attorney:	Stother, George F.; Cozens, Horatio
Verdict:	Not freed
Notes:	

Plaintiff under age twenty-one; by her next friend and lawyer James H. Peck, filed a plea against the defendant claiming he had imprisoned her for eighty days at his house, and another twenty-five days at a location forty miles down the Mississippi River; included affidavit from Peck naming David Jack as plaintiff's next friend in previous suit filed in February; requested Francois Valois and defendant to be held in contempt for removing plaintiff to Ste. Genevieve and attempting to sell plaintiff in New Orleans outside jurisdiction of the court.

1822

Plaintiff:	Susan
Defendant:	Hight, Henry
Plaintiff's Attorney:	McGirk, Matthias; Benton
Defendant's Attorney:	Barton, Joshua; Easton, Rufus; Pettibone, Rufus
Verdict:	Not freed
Notes:	

Plaintiff was once a slave of James Reyan, also spelled Reyal, Rayal, Rayan, Rain; Reyan moved plaintiff from Maryland to Indiana Territory, in what became northern Illinois; defendant was administrator to Reyan's estate; originally filed in St. Charles Circuit Court; appealed to Missouri Supreme Court; included recognizance bond put up by McGirk, plaintiff's attorney; transcript of case for Missouri Supreme Court; testimony for plaintiff by McGirk and William B. Whitesides.

1822

Plaintiff:	Jeffrie
Defendant:	Robidoux, Joseph
Plaintiff's Attorney:	Wash, Robert; [Pettus, Spencer]; Bird, Gustavus A.; Geyer, Henry S.
Defendant's Attorney:	Strother, George F.; Cozens, Horatio
Verdict:	N/A
Notes:	

Plaintiff name also spelled Jeffrey; entered a plea of trespass by next friend and grandmother Rachael Camp, also spelled Camph, and attorney Robert Wash; included document in French; motion to dismiss trial stating plaintiff should not have had next friend since not stated being under age of twenty-one; affidavit from Camp alleging plaintiff was under twenty-one at time of original filing of suit; change of venue to Jefferson County; change of venue revoked back to St. Louis; document from Missouri Supreme Court justices investigating plaintiff's movement for reversing dismissal; transcript of case listed jurors; jurors included Louis C. Benoist, George H.C. Melody, and Paul M. Gratiot.

1823

Plaintiff:	Malinda
Defendant:	Wilburn, Robert
Plaintiff's Attorney:	N/A
Defendant's Attorney:	Strother, George F.; Cozens, Horatio
Verdict:	N/A
Notes:	

Plaintiff's petition coupled with her daughter's, Nelly, October Term 1823 case #8; claimed defendant moved to Illinois taking the plaintiff with him; she lived there about five months until defendant moved her to Missouri; plaintiff alleged defendant moved her to prevent her filing a suit in Illinois; next friend Beriah Clelland; included affidavit requesting writ of habeas corpus; jury instructions included Nelly's case.

1823

Plaintiff:	Fenwick, Lethe
Defendant:	Abbott, Samuel
Plaintiff's Attorney:	Strother, George F.; Cozens, Hortatio
Defendant's Attorney:	Geyer, Henry S.
Verdict:	N/A
Notes:	

Plaintiff name also spelled Letty; filed suit of trespass and assault against defendant; defendant claimed he was not guilty of assault on grounds plaintiff was a servant and slave at the time of the beating, and "refused to obey lawful commands"; accused plaintiff of behaving improperly and being "saucy," crimes punishable when committed by a slave.

1823

Plaintiff:	Nelly
Defendant:	Wilburn, Robert
Plaintiff's Attorney:	N/A
Defendant's Attorney:	Strother, George F.; Cozens, Horatio
Verdict:	Not freed

Notes:

Plaintiff through next friend Beriah Clelland filed plea of trespass against defendant; daughter of Malinda, October Term 1823 case #7; petition filed for both Malinda and Nelly; Clelland claimed defendant was still a resident of Illinois; alleged defendant prevented Nelly and Malinda from filing suit in Illinois by moving them to Missouri.

1825

Plaintiff:	Harry
Defendant:	Pettibone, Rufus; Hatton, Charles; Wingfield, Owen; Voteau, Isaac; Butler, John; Whitset, Sanford
Plaintiff's Attorney:	Bates, Edward; McGirk, Isaac C.
Defendant's Attorney:	Spalding, Josiah; Cozens, Horatio
Verdict:	N/A

Notes:

Plaintiff by next friend Alexander Clark filed a plea of trespass; claimed damages of $500; defendants with last name Whitset also known as Whitesides.

1825

Plaintiff:	Malinda
Defendant:	Pettibone, Rufus; Hatton, Charles; Wingfield, Owen; Voteau, Isaac; Butler, John; Whitset, Sanford
Plaintiff's Attorney:	Bates, Edward; McGirk, Isaac C.
Defendant's Attorney:	Spalding, Josiah; Cozens, Horatio
Verdict:	Freed

Notes:

Plaintiff by next friend Alexander Clark filed a plea of trespass; claimed damages of $500; defendants with last name Whitset also known as Whitesides; Rufus Pettibone deceased by time of suit; Levi Pettibone administrator to estate.

1825

Plaintiff:	Jenny
Defendant:	Musick, Ephraim; Hatton, Charles; Wingfield, Owen; Voteau, Isaac; Butler, John; Whitset; Sanford
Plaintiff's Attorney:	Bates, Edward; McGirk, Isaac C.; Farris, R. T.
Defendant's Attorney:	Spalding, Josiah; Cozens, Horatio

Verdict: Freed

Notes:

Included affidavit for continuance by defendant citing Applegate as material witness; notice by defendant Ephraim Musick stating witness Robert Musick had not received his summons; defendants with last name Whitset also known as Whitesides.

1825

Plaintiff:	Lorinda
Defendant:	Pettibone, Rufus; Hatton, Charles; Wingfield, Owen; Voteau, Isaac; Butler, John; Whitset, Sanford
Plaintiff's Attorney:	Bates, Edward; McGirk, Isaac C.
Defendant's Attorney:	Spalding, Josiah
Verdict:	N/A

Notes:

Plaintiff by next friend Alexander Clark filed plea of trespass; claimed damages of $500; defendants with last name Whitset also known as Whitesides; Rufus Pettibone deceased by time of suit; Levi Pettibone administrator to estate.

1825

Plaintiff:	Winetta (Winny)
Defendant:	Musick, Ephraim; Hatton, Charles; Wingfield, Owen; Voteau, Isaac; Butler, John; Whitset, Sanford
Plaintiff's Attorney:	Bates, Edward; McGirk, Isaac C.; Farris, R. T.
Defendant's Attorney:	Cozens, Horatio
Verdict:	Freed

Notes:

Plaintiff also called Winney; by next friend Alexander Clark filed plea of trespass against defendants; claimed damages of $500; defendants with last name also known as Whitesides; summons issued for Daniel Applegate noted sheriff believed him to be dead.

1825

Plaintiff:	Winny
Defendant:	Pettibone, Rufus; Hatton, Charles; Wingfield, Owen; Voteau, Isaac; Butler, John; Whitset, Sanford
Plaintiff's Attorney:	Bates, Edward; McGirk, Isaac C.

Defendant's Attorney: Spalding, Josiah; Cozens, Horatio
Verdict: N/A
Notes:

Plaintiff's name also spelled Winne, Winney; by next friend Alexander Clark filed plea of trespass; defendants with last name Whitset, also known as Whitesides; bill of exceptions mentioned Winny's residence in Illinois at age twelve or fourteen with owner John Whitset; mentioned Thomas, who claimed Winny after John's death; included agreement between lawyers to use same depositions in Winny's case with cases of Malinda, Harry, Lorinda, Jinny, and Winetta; Rufus Pettibone deceased by time of suit; Levi Pettibone administrator to estate.

1825

Plaintiff: Marguerite
Defendant: Chouteau, Pierre, Sr.
Plaintiff's Attorney: Farris, [R. T.]; McGirk, [Isaac]; Gamble, [Hamilton]
Defendant's Attorney: Cozens, Horatio; Spalding, Josiah; Bates, Edward;
                Geyer, Henry S.; Lawless, [Luke E.]
Verdict: Freed
Notes:

Plaintiff's name also spelled Margaritte; by next friend, Pierre Baribeau, filed suit of trespass against defendant; claimed damages of $500.

1826

Plaintiff: Israel
Defendant: Rector, William
Plaintiff's Attorney: Strother, George F.
Defendant's Attorney: McGirk, Isaac C. (attorney for Isaac Letcher)
Verdict: Freed
Notes:

Plaintiff through next friend Augustus H. Evans sued for freedom; claimed defendant took him into Illinois to reside for several months at a time at family plantation; requested for writ of habeas corpus to prevent his sale by Sheriff John K. Walker; to be sold to satisfy several executions against Rector; Isaac A. Letcher impleaded as defendant after purchasing plaintiff at sale; gave statement that he believed Israel entitled to his freedom.

1826

Plaintiff:	Dorinda
Defendant:	Simonds, John, Jr.
Plaintiff's Attorney:	Cozens, Horatio
Defendant's Attorney:	Geyer, Henry S.
Verdict:	Not freed

Notes:

Plaintiff claimed owner Avington Phelps moved her to Illinois, where she resided for about two years; Phelps then moved her to St. Louis and mortgaged her to John Simonds Jr.; deposition by Richard Hamilton claimed Phelps did not intend for plaintiff to live in Illinois, but meant to hire her out in Missouri; included letter from Simonds to Phelps notifying him of the suit; affidavit for continuance from Phelps to gain a material witness currently in "Spanish territory" in Texas.

1826

Plaintiff:	State of Missouri
Defendant:	Walker, John K.; Chouteau, Pierre; Pratt, Bernard; Amelin, Alexis
Plaintiff's Attorney:	Habeas Corpus
Defendant's Attorney:	N/A
Verdict:	N/A

Notes:

Included order to explain the imprisonment of four "persons of colour," Catiche alias Catherine, Julie, Helen, and Joseph; affidavit from defendant Amelin; claimed he was not owner of said Catherine, Helen, or Julie but was acting as agent for Alexander Scott, a "master" of the steam boat "General Brown"; claimed he was ordered by Scott to bring the three women before Robert Wash, justice of Missouri Supreme Court, on writ of habeas corpus; Wash in St. Charles upon arrival, so Amelin put them in custody of Walker, jailor of St. Louis; claimed Joseph was slave of Pierre Chouteau; believed Chouteau had moved Joseph to a location up the Missouri River; mentioned Herculaneum in Jefferson County, Missouri.

1826

Plaintiff:	Jenny
Defendant:	Musick, Robert
Plaintiff's Attorney:	N/A

Defendant's Attorney: N/A
Verdict: Freed
Notes:

Order to sheriff to revive judgment for the plaintiff to collect eighty-five dollars for damages sustained in trespass and costs awarded by previous suit; judgment had not yet been executed; defendant could not be found.

1826

Plaintiff: Merry, John
Defendant: Tiffin, Clayton; Menard, Louis
Plaintiff's Attorney: Charless, Joseph; McGirk, Isaac C.
Defendant's Attorney: Lawless, [Luke E.]; Bates, Edward
Verdict: Freed
Notes:

Plaintiff also called Jean Marie in depositions of witnesses; age thirty-five or thirty-six; claimed born a slave in Cahokia, Illinois, after the Ordinance of 1787; Pensino, also Peceneau and Piceneau, claimed plaintiff and his parents as slaves; sold plaintiff to his son Lewis Piceneau; verbal contract between Lewis and plaintiff for purchasing his freedom for $450 to be paid in three years; claimed paid Piceneau $200 and two horses for total of $230 before the three year period expired; Piceneau gave him freedom to work off rest of money; plaintiff moved to St. Louis where siezed on Piceneau's orders and taken by steam boat to New Orleans; sold to Andrew Shecksni, from whom he "absconded" and returned to Cahokia; recaptured and brought to St. Louis, where posessed by defendants; depositions mentioned steam boat *General Brown* on which plaintiff was bound in irons; first bill of exceptions stated plaintiff had verbal contract to purchase not only himself but his wife and two children for $900; Supreme Court Justice granted new trial in circuit court; included second bill of instructions and jury instructions.

1826

Plaintiff: Jerry
Defendant: Hatton, Charles
Plaintiff's Attorney: N/A
Defendant's Attorney: N/A
Verdict: N/A
Notes:

Order to sheriff to revive judgment for the plaintiff to collect $170 for damages sustained in trespass and costs awarded by previous suit; judgment had not yet been executed; defendant could not be found.

1826

Plaintiff:	Jefferson, Joseph
Defendant:	McCutchen, William; McKnight, James
Plaintiff's Attorney:	Charless, Joseph; McGirk, Isaac C.
Defendant's Attorney:	Bates, Edward
Verdict:	Not freed
Notes:	

Plaintiff twenty-seven years old; claimed born a slave to a slave mother and free white father, Thomas Jefferson, in Virginia; Jefferson, his father and master, sold plaintiff at age four to defendant James McKnight; alleged McKnight purchased him on condition plaintiff would be free at age twenty-one; McKnight brought plaintiff to Missouri, where sold to his father, Timothy McKnight; at Timothy's death, plaintiff passed into ownership of other defendant, William McCutcheon; denied his freedom despite being over age of twenty-one.

1827

Plaintiff:	LaGrange, Francois
Defendant:	Pratte, Bernard; Chouteau, Pierre; Berthold, Bartholomew; Cabanne, Jean P.
Plaintiff's Attorney:	Charless, Joseph; Lawless, Luke E.; Strother, George F.
Defendant's Attorney:	Geyer, Henry S.
Verdict:	Not freed
Notes:	

Plaintiff also called Isidore, or Isadore; claimed born in St. Louis as a slave of Pascal Cerre; Cerre sold him to Pierre Menard of Kaskaskia, Illinois; Menard took him to Illinois where he lived for two or three months; Menard then hired him out as a hand on board a boat bound for New Orleans; worked on boat for about six months; brought back to Illinois for about three months; taken to St. Louis and sold to defendants; bill of exceptions and testimony of Menard mentioned the boat plaintiff worked on was a keel boat; Menard claimed he had not purchased plaintiff for himself from Cerre because he lived in Illinois, but had purchased him for Chouteau, a resident of St. Louis; Menard mentioned Mine La Motte in southern Missouri where plaintiff worked; Jean Cabanne also called John.

1827

Plaintiff:	Wilson, Polly
Defendant:	Baum, Jacob
Plaintiff's Attorney:	Strother, George F.
Defendant's Attorney:	Magenis, Arthur L.
Verdict:	N/A
Notes:	

Plaintiff filed plea of trespass against the defendant; claimed defendant beat her about her head, back, face, and other parts with a stick, whip, and his fists; damages $500.

1827

Plaintiff:	Milly
Defendant:	Smith, Stephen
Plaintiff's Attorney:	Spalding, Josiah
Defendant's Attorney:	Geyer, Henry S.; Magenis, Arthur S.
Verdict:	Freed
Notes:	

Petition for plaintiff, Harry, Dick, William, David Shipman, and the unnamed infant of plaintiff; claimed owner David Shipman moved them to Indiana from Kentucky; in Indiana, claimed emancipated; moved with Shipman to Tarewell County, Illinois, to live with him as free people; claimed defendant kidnapped them and brought as slaves to St. Louis; defendant claimed Shipman had mortgaged siezed slaves to repay defendant for debt on which defendant was security; included mortgage contract between Shipman and defendant; mentioned Milly's husband Moses, and two daughters Ann Maria and Mary Ann; David Shipman on petition, also Davey, Milly's son; also mentioned slaves Sarah and Eliza; included bill of exceptions; transcript for Missouri Supreme Court; depositions for Shelbyville, Kentucky, and Peoria, Illinois.

1827

Plaintiff:	Dick, Harry
Defendant:	Smith, Stephen
Plaintiff's Attorney:	Spalding, Josiah
Defendant's Attorney:	Geyer, Henry S.
Verdict:	N/A

Notes:

Plaintiff filed a plea of trespass; alleged defendant beat and bruised him; sought damages of $500; judge, while on vacation, permitted plaintiff to sue; mentioned Milly, William, and David Shipman.

1827

Plaintiff:	William
Defendant:	Smith, Stephen
Plaintiff's Attorney:	Spalding, Josiah
Defendant's Attorney:	Geyer, Henry S.
Verdict:	N/A

Notes:

Plaintiff filed a plea of trespass; alleged defendant beat and bruised him; sought damages of $500; judge's permission to sue included Milly, Harry, Dick, and David Shipman besides the plaintiff.

1827

Plaintiff:	Shipman, David
Defendant:	Smith, Stephen
Plaintiff's Attorney:	Spalding, Josiah
Defendant's Attorney:	Geyer, Henry S.
Verdict:	N/A

Notes:

Plaintiff filed a plea of trespass; alleged defendant beat and bruised him; sought damages of $500; judge's permission to sue included Milly, Harry, Dick, and William besides the plaintiff.

1827

Plaintiff:	Rector, Molly
Defendant:	Bivens, John
Plaintiff's Attorney:	Charless, Joseph
Defendant's Attorney:	N/A
Verdict:	N/A

Notes:

Plaintiff born in Kentucky; owned by John Thruston; Thruston gave to daughter Francis upon her marriage to Col. Elias Rector; taken to Kaskaskia, Illinois, where lived for four or five years; claimed Rector promised to emancipate her if faithfully serve him for four years; lived in St. Louis three or four years; worked for six months for brother-in-law Joseph Barton; sold to brother Stephen Rector with same condition of four years; Elias died; taken by Stephen to St. Clair County, Illinois; Wharton Rector took to St. Louis and sold to defendant; brought suit by next friend Louis A. Benoist.

1827

Plaintiff:	Mary
Defendant:	Menard, Francis; Landreville, Andre
Plaintiff's Attorney:	McGirk, Isaac C.; Bass, John N.
Defendant's Attorney:	Strother, George F.
Verdict:	N/A
Notes:	

Plaintiff claimed to be born in Kaskaskia, Illinois; owned by Michel Bevenue; after Bevenue's death, sold to Francois Menard; brought to St. Louis about three years prior to suit; in custody of Landeville; petition included daughters Virginia, age seven, Victoire, age six, and Elisabeth, age three.

1827

Plaintiff:	Theotiste
Defendant:	Chouteau, Pierre, Jr.
Plaintiff's Attorney:	Darby, John F.
Defendant's Attorney:	Hempstead, Charles S.
Verdict:	Not freed
Notes:	

Plaintiff also called Catiche; claimed born in Praire Du Rocher, Illinois; owned by W. Bourbeau; at his death, sold to Manuel Lisa in the Territory of Missouri; after Lisa's death, sold to defendant; affidavit from John B. Sarpy asking for continuance on part of defendant to obtain record of birth and baptism from Prairie du Rocher; included application from plaintiff to appeal case to Supreme Court; bill of exceptions marked plaintiff's birth in 1782.

1827

Plaintiff:	Elizabeth
Defendant:	Menard, Francis; Landreville, Andre
Plaintiff's Attorney:	McGirk, Isaac C.; Bass, John N.

Defendant's Attorney: Strother, George F.

Verdict: Not freed

Notes:

Plaintiff permitted by court to sue by Alexis Amelin, her next friend; damages $500.

1827

Plaintiff: Virginia

Defendant: Menard, Francis; Landreville, Andre

Plaintiff's Attorney: McGirk, Isaac C.; Bass, John N.

Defendant's Attorney: Strother, George F.

Verdict: Not freed

Notes:

Plaintiff permitted by court to sue by Alexis Amelin, her next friend; damages $500.

1827

Plaintiff: Singleton, John

Defendant: Scott, Alexander; Lewis, Robert

Plaintiff's Attorney: McGirk, Isaac C.

Defendant's Attorney: Geyer, Henry S.

Verdict: Freed

Notes:

Plaintiff claimed to be born of a free mother in Illinois; mother Philis Singleton had been emancipated by her owner Ogle prior to the birth of plaintiff; after reaching adulthood, kidnapped by Jeptha Lamkins and sold in Alabama to Zechariah Neal; attempted to sue for freedom there, but taken to New Orleans by Henry Byron before suit was decided; bought by Robert Lewis in New Orleans; escaped to St. Louis by steamboat *America*; arrested and imprisoned on order of steamboat captain, Alexander Scott.

1827

Plaintiff: Victoire

Defendant: Menard, Francis; Landreville, Andre

Plaintiff's Attorney: McGirk, Isaac C.; Bass, John N.

Defendant's Attorney: Strother, George F.

Verdict: Not freed

Notes:

Plaintiff permitted by court to sue by Alexis Amelin, her next friend; damages $500.

1827

Plaintiff:	Aspasia
Defendant:	Chouteau, Francois; Menard, Pierre
Plaintiff's Attorney:	McGuire, Isaac C.; Bent, John
Defendant's Attorney:	Spalding, Josiah
Verdict:	N/A
Notes:	

Plaintiff also called Aspasie; claimed born in Kaskaskia, Illinois, to Negro mother in 1806; held in slavery by Baptiste Jeandreau; sold to Col. Pierre Menard five years earlier; given to Francois Chouteau and his wife, Menard's daughter who lived in St. Louis; included affidavit alleging defendant about to move her downriver by steamboat *America*.

1828

Plaintiff:	Dolly
Defendant:	Young, John
Plaintiff's Attorney:	Strother, George F.; Evans, James
Defendant's Attorney:	McGirk, [Isaac C.]
Verdict:	Not freed
Notes:	

Plaintiff, about forty, claimed defendant forcibly removed her to Feever River mines [now Galena River] in Northwest Territory [now Galena, Illinois, and southwest Wisconsin], holding her there for six months; included writ of habeas corpus to produce Dolly; recognizance bond by defendant and Douglas Ferguson for $400 each.

1828

Plaintiff:	Aspasia
Defendant:	Chouteau, Francois; Menard, Pierre
Plaintiff's Attorney:	McGirk, Isaac C.; Bent, John
Defendant's Attorney:	Allen, Beverly
Verdict:	Freed
Notes:	

Plaintiff claimed to have been born in Kaskaskia, Illinois, around year 1806; owned by Baptiste Gendreau until his death; sold to Peter or Pierre Menard; given by Menard to his daughter Therise and son-in-law Francois Chouteau; included bill of exceptions with jury instructions.

1828

Plaintiff:	Peter
Defendant:	Walton, James
Plaintiff's Attorney:	Strother, George F.
Defendant's Attorney:	Geyer, Henry S.
Verdict:	Not freed
Notes:	

Plaintiff, also known as Peter Jackson, claimed born a slave; owned by William Walton; given to Edward Lansford and Betsy, Edward's wife and Walton's daughter; the Lansfords took plaintiff to Illinois; brought to Missouri by Henry Walton; came into hands of defendant; included $500 recognizance bond; affidavit for new trial.

1828

Plaintiff:	Matilda
Defendant:	Rocheblave, Philip; Rocheblave, Mary Louisa
Plaintiff's Attorney:	Darby, John F.
Defendant's Attorney:	Geyer, Henry S.
Verdict:	Freed
Notes:	

Plaintiff born in Prairie du Rocher, Illinois, in 1806 or 1807; owned by Susan Lecount, or Lecompt; delivered over to Philip Rocheblave and moved to St. Louis; included special verdict which noted Rocheblave was Lecount's son-in-law.

1828

Plaintiff:	Edmund
Defendant:	Reynolds, John
Plaintiff's Attorney:	Charless, Joseph
Defendant's Attorney:	N/A
Verdict:	N/A
Notes:	

Plaintiff filed plea of trespass against owner and defendant through next friend; claimed $100 damages; sheriff noted defendant not found in the county.

1828

Plaintiff:	Relfe, George
Defendant:	Ficklin, Thompson H.

Plaintiff's Attorney:	Geyer, Henry S.
Defendant's Attorney:	Gamble, Hamilton R.
Verdict:	N/A
Notes:	

Plaintiff's last name also spelled Relf; claimed born a slave in Virginia; owned by James Duff who gave plaintiff to his daughter and her husband, James H. Relfe; Relfe took plaintiff from Virginia to Ste. Genevieve, Missouri, and then Illinois, where resided two years; alleged James H. had entered agreement with George, at age seventeen, to indenture himself till he reached age twenty-eight; George, who could not read, signed agreement only to learn the term was actually ninety-nine years; claimed James H. set him free a few years later in Missouri, admitting contract was invalid; George then siezed after several months of freedom as slave of James Duff; sold by Dr. Lewis Linn of Ste. Genevieve to Augustus Jones; then sold to defendant with proceeds from sale going to James H. Relfe; deposition from James H. claimed indenture was fifty years, George was borrowed from Duff, and George was a runaway several months after trying to "commit murder" on Relfe's family and slaves; included document in French.

1828

Plaintiff:	John
Defendant:	Reynolds, John
Plaintiff's Attorney:	Charless, Joseph
Defendant's Attorney:	N/A
Verdict:	N/A
Notes:	

Plaintiff filed plea of trespass against owner and defendant through next friend; claimed $100 damages; sheriff noted defendant not found in the county; John born in Illinois, son of Suzette; Suzette was held in the possession of Julie Jarrot, McCracken, Louis Pincinneau, and John Reynolds, all in Illinois.

1828

Plaintiff:	Angelique
Defendant:	Reynolds, John
Plaintiff's Attorney:	Charless, Joseph
Defendant's Attorney:	N/A
Verdict:	N/A

Notes:

Plaintiff filed plea of trespass against owner and defendant through next friend; claimed $100 damages; sheriff noted defendant not found in the county.

1829

Plaintiff:	Suzette
Defendant:	Reynolds, John
Plaintiff's Attorney:	Charless, Joseph
Defendant's Attorney:	N/A
Verdict:	N/A

Notes:

Plaintiff, about twenty-five, also called Judith Bequette and Suzette Mary; petitioned for her and her children's freedom; John, age eight; Angelique, age two; Edmund, two months old; claimed born in Ste. Genevieve in family of Nicholas Beauvois; after Nicholas's death, given to his daughter Julie Jarrot of Cahokia, Illinois; Jarrot transferred and sold her to son-in-law McCracken; sold to Louis Pincinneau; sold to defendant; claimed children had all been born since her original residence in Illinois.

1829

Plaintiff:	Simpson, Robert
Defendant:	Strother, George F.
Plaintiff's Attorney:	McGirk, Isaac C.
Defendant's Attorney:	Magenis, Arthur S.
Verdict:	N/A

Notes:

Plaintiff was sheriff; sued Strother for failing to pay bond on which Strother was principal; bond was for hiring Aspasia during her suit against Francois Chouteau; plaintiff claimed Strother owed $500 for bond, and $47.065 for term of hire; Strother claimed Aspasia had been awarded her freedom and written him clear of any charges; also claimed to have already paid the sum for the term of hire.

1829

Plaintiff:	Virginia
Defendant:	Menard, Francis
Plaintiff's Attorney:	N/A
Defendant's Attorney:	N/A

Verdict: N/A
Notes:

Summons for Menard to appear in court to answer plaintiff's plea of trespass and damages of $500; plaintiff's next friend Alexis Amelin; sheriff unable to locate Menard.

1829

Plaintiff:	Elizabeth
Defendant:	Menard, Francis
Plaintiff's Attorney:	McGirk, Isaac C.; Bass, John N.
Defendant's Attorney:	N/A
Verdict:	N/A

Notes:

Summons for Menard to appear in court to answer plaintiff's plea of trespass and damages of $500; plaintiff's next friend Alexis Amelin; sheriff unable to locate Menard.

1829

Plaintiff:	Mary
Defendant:	Menard, Francis
Plaintiff's Attorney:	N/A
Defendant's Attorney:	N/A
Verdict:	Not freed

Notes:

Summons for Menard to appear in court to answer plaintiff's plea of trespass and damages of $500; sheriff unable to locate Menard.

1829

Plaintiff:	Victoire
Defendant:	Menard, Francis
Plaintiff's Attorney:	N/A
Defendant's Attorney:	N/A
Verdict:	Not freed

Notes:

Summons for Menard to appear in court to answer plaintiff's plea of trespass and damages of $500; plaintiff's next friend Alexis Amelin; sheriff unable to locate

Menard.

1829

Plaintiff:	Vincent
Defendant:	Jerry (Duncan)
Plaintiff's Attorney:	Bird, Gustavus A.
Defendant's Attorney:	N/A
Verdict:	Not freed
Notes:	

Plaintiff hired out to defendant by Coleman Duncan, agent for John Duncan, Vincent's owner in Kentucky; claimed previous owner Jesse Duncan, John's father, hired Vincent out in Illinois from 1816 or 1817 till 1819 when he died; John, who claimed Vincent after Jesse's death, kept him in Illinois till 1826; defendant also known as Jerry Duncan.

1829

Plaintiff:	Peter
Defendant:	Walton, James
Plaintiff's Attorney:	Edwards, John C.
Defendant's Attorney:	Geyer, Henry S.
Verdict:	N/A
Notes:	

Plaintiff claimed born in North Carolina, the property of William Walton; Walton moved to Missouri with plaintiff nearly twenty-one years earlier; one year after move, gave plaintiff to his daughter, Elisabeth, wife of Edward Lunsford; Lunsford lived in Illinois and kept plaintiff there two years; now held by James Walton in St. Louis; affidavit from plaintiff claiming he was being punished for bringing suit; included affidavit for continuance; bill of exceptions mentioned continuance denied; affidavit for appeal.

1829

Plaintiff:	Jones, Nicholas
Defendant:	Honey, John W.; Gray, John
Plaintiff's Attorney:	Coulter, John D.
Defendant's Attorney:	Bates, Edward
Verdict:	Freed

Notes:

Plaintiff born a slave in Maryland; claimed previous owner Trueman Tyler had emancipated him; depositions mentioned plaintiff's father, Aaron Jones, a free man of color, had placed plaintiff as a laborer on board a "vessel" to "[break] certain bad habits"; vessel's captain named John Johnson sailed from Annapolis to New Orleans; also mentioned plaintiff's mother, also a slave of Tyler, died shortly after his birth.

1829

Plaintiff:	Ewton, Carey
Defendant:	Wilder, Benjamin
Plaintiff's Attorney:	Darby, John F.
Defendant's Attorney:	Magenis, Arthur S.
Verdict:	Not freed

Notes:

Plaintiff last name also spelled Ooton; born a slave in the family of Robertson in Petersburg, Virginia, around 1790; sold on an execution against Robertson to Richard Cox; taken to Springfield, Kentucky; sold to John Hughes, who sent plaintiff to Palmyra, Missouri, with Thomas Hughes; Thomas moved plaintiff to Galena, Illinois, to work in the Fever River lead mines; moved back to Palmyra, where sold to William Mulder; Mulder immediately took plaintiff to St. Charles where sold to William Ewton, alias Ooton; slave of Ewton until his death; sold as property of estate to Benjamin Wilder; included writ of habeas corpus.

1829

Plaintiff:	Whiten, Maria
Defendant:	Rucker, Garland
Plaintiff's Attorney:	Strother, George F.; Newman, John
Defendant's Attorney:	Gamble, Hamilton R.
Verdict:	Not freed

Notes:

Plaintiff also called Mariah; had infant son named Patrick Henry; claimed born a slave in Bedford County, Virginia; property of Jesse Whiten, also Whitten; moved with plaintiff and her child to Kentucky for two months; moved to Illinois where hired her out to Abraham Granger; there only three months when Whiten died; alleged Whiten had emancipated plaintiff and her child in front of witnesses on his death bed; lived as a free woman for a period of time before taken by defendant and claimed as a slave; depositions from Jesse's father, William, and neighbor Jacob Fizor claimed Jesse had not owned plaintiff, but had "absconded" with her; Fizor's testimony alleged Jesse kept plaintiff as his "wife" and had fathered Patrick Henry; claimed legitimate owner was Abel B. Nichols, who had purchased her at a sale in Virginia.

1829

Plaintiff:	Henry, Patrick
Defendant:	Rucker, Garland
Plaintiff's Attorney:	Strother, George F.
Defendant's Attorney:	Gamble, Hamilton R.
Verdict:	Not freed

Notes:

Plaintiff sued by next friend and mother, Maria Whiten; claimed born a slave in Virginia; property of Jesse Whiten; Whiten moved plaintiff and Maria to Kentucky for two months; moved then to Illinois where hired out Maria to Abraham Granger; alleged Whiten died three months later, emancipating both mother and child on his death bed.

1829

Plaintiff:	Vincent
Defendant:	Duncan, James
Plaintiff's Attorney:	Bird, Gustavus A.; Gamble, Hamilton R.
Defendant's Attorney:	Bates, Edward
Verdict:	Freed

Notes:

Plaintiff had filed previous suit against John Duncan; filed new suit since Coleman and James Duncan had recently claimed him as a slave as well; believed James was attempting to take plaintiff to New Orleans and sell him; claimed formerly a slave of Jesse Duncan, deceased; around 1815 or 1816, Jesse took plaintiff to Illinois from Kentucky; around 1819, Jesse died; his heirs kept plaintiff hired out in Illinois; at end of 1826, James brought plaintiff to Missouri to hire him out; included warrant for Coleman's slaves Joe and Ralph, who he claimed ran away; deposition of Reason Neighswonger described plaintiff's work in saline saltworks in Illinois; mentioned Bob Smith, a black man, and Robert M. Funkhouser who both hired plaintiff; included judgements of Supreme Court to retry case at Circuit Court level; included list of jurors; bill of exception mentioned testimonies not included in depositions; also included copy of 6th article of Illinois's state constitution.

1830

Plaintiff:	Joe
Defendant:	Duncan, Coleman; Duncan, James
Plaintiff's Attorney:	Spalding, Josiah
Defendant's Attorney:	Bates, Edward
Verdict:	Not freed

Notes:

Plaintiff claimed to have been held a slave for the past eleven years by defendants; taken three years earlier with Coleman's knowledge from Kentucky to Galena, Illinois, to work; had been hired out before then for six or seven years consecutively to work for two or three months at a time at the salt works in Illinois; had brought suit in Galena against James, but defeated as Coleman was proved to be his legal owner; expected defendants to take him to Alabama to sell him out of the jurisdiction of the court.

1830

Plaintiff:	Henry, William
Defendant:	Bates, David G.
Plaintiff's Attorney:	Spalding, Josiah
Defendant's Attorney:	Bates, Edward
Verdict:	N/A

Notes:

Plaintiff age thirty-one; claimed born in Virginia and brought to Kaskaskia, Illinois, at age fifteen; sold to Huge Maxwell, a permanent resident; lived with Maxwell for eleven years when sold to Daniel Dunklin of Washington County, Missouri; sold to Elijah Inge, who took him to Galena, Illinois; sold to William Hempstead, who kept plaintiff in Galena until three months prior to his suit; sold to defendant who brought plaintiff to St. Louis; defendant the captain of a steamboat; plaintiff worked as fireman on boat; Bates not resident of St. Louis; plaintiff in danger of being removed from jurisdiction of court on boat.

1830

Plaintiff:	Ralph
Defendant:	Duncan, Coleman; Duncan, James
Plaintiff's Attorney:	Bird, Gustavus A.
Defendant's Attorney:	Bates, Edward
Verdict:	Freed

Notes:

Plaintiff alleged he had resided and worked in Illinois and Michigan Territory for more than two years; while in Illinois, he claimed to have started suit against James Duncan, but case was dismissed as Coleman Duncan was considered owner of plaintiff; while waiting for Coleman to be served by new suit, plaintiff claimed he was kidnapped by James and brought to St. Louis; threatened with being "put in irons" and sold in Kentucky; plaintiff had tried to purchase his freedom, but Coleman had refused; depositions place plaintiff at Fever River lead mines and Saline Licks in Illinois; deposition mapped out Ralph's ownership history: owned first by John Gordon, sold to Iassac Metcalfe, sold to Abner West, who sold plaintiff to defendant Coleman Duncan.

1830

Plaintiff:	Matilda
Defendant:	St. Vrain, Charles
Plaintiff's Attorney:	Bird, Gustavus A.
Defendant's Attorney:	N/A
Verdict:	N/A

Notes:

Plaintiff under the age of twenty-one, sued by next friend and mother, Sarah; claimed mother was free when she was born on March 16, 1810; born four miles south of Edwardsville, Illinois, where she resided until two months prior to the suit; claimed defendant took her from Illinois to St. Ferdinand in St. Louis County, where he held her as a slave; claimed $300 damages.

1831

Plaintiff:	Cary
Defendant:	Wilder, Benjamin
Plaintiff's Attorney:	Steele, John; Bird, Gustavus A.
Defendant's Attorney:	Gamble, Hamilton R.

Verdict:	Not freed
Notes:	

Plaintiff name also spelled Carey; claimed taken to Galena, Illinois, by previous owner Thomas J. Hughes to work in mines; hired out for three weeks to individuals and another three weeks "digging minerals"; defendant claimed title to plaintiff through Hughes; plaintiff believed he was in danger of being sold to "some distant place"; affidavit for new trial by plaintiff noted he had missed preparing for his case because he was hired out to Capt. Enoch Price of the steamboat *St. Louis* to travel to New Orleans and back; meant to ask for continuance, but fell sick and missed court date; claimed defendant failed to provide him with adequate food and clothing and forced plaintiff to continue to work despite his illness; included bill of exceptions.

1831

Plaintiff:	Peter
Defendant:	Walton, James
Plaintiff's Attorney:	Stother, George F.
Defendant's Attorney:	Geyer, Henry S.
Verdict:	Not freed
Notes:	

Plaintiff born in North Carolina; owner William Walton moved him to St. Louis approximately twenty-three years earlier; sent to live with Walton's daughter Elizabeth Lunsford two years later; lived with Lunsford in Indiana for two years; came back to St. Louis and claimed by defendant; plaintiff requested deposition by John T. Walton to be included in his petition; John claimed William had admitted before his death that plaintiff entitled to his freedom.

1831

Plaintiff:	Dunky
Defendant:	Hay, Andrew
Plaintiff's Attorney:	Shaw, George D.; Foreman, Stephen W.; Bates, [Edward]
Defendant's Attorney:	Gamble, Hamilton R.
Verdict:	Not freed
Notes:	

Plaintiff claimed born in Africa; landed in Charleston, South Carolina, twenty years prior to her suit; moved by Alcorn Beard and James Bryant to Kaskaskia, Illinois;

delivered to William Morrison; served as indentured servant until April 1831; moved her to St. Louis; defendant claimed plaintiff had escaped to St. Louis, that she was there without his permission; included bill of exceptions, which described arrest of plaintiff as accused runaway; included depositions.

1831

Plaintiff:	Julia
Defendant:	McKenney, Samuel T.
Plaintiff's Attorney:	Strother, George F.; Bird, Gustavus A.
Defendant's Attorney:	Shaw, George D.; Gamble, Hamilton R.
Verdict:	Freed

Notes:

Plaintiff born in Tennessee; owned by Asa Carrington who moved to Montgomery County, Kentucky prior to his death; his widow Lucinda and his son Joseph emigrated with plaintiff to Pike County, Illinois, and kept plaintiff; after residing in Illinois for approximately eight weeks, plaintiff was taken to Louisiana, Pike County, Missouri, where hired out for nine months; returned with Joseph to Illinois, where stayed in Pike County, Illinois, for five weeks and three days; taken by Joseph to St. Louis where sold to defendant; numerous depositions from Louisiana, Missouri, and Pike County, Illinois; depositions stated plaintiff had been hired by Dr. Abraham Stewart in Louisiana, Missouri; some claimed Lucinda had not intended to reside in Illinois with plaintiff; mentioned Julia's daughter Harriet; included transcript from Missouri Supreme Court with judgement for a new trial; transcript cited *Winny v. Whiteside*; discussed the legality of "passing through" free territory with slave property; later depositions questioned the character of numerous witnesses as well as the character of attorney Gustavus A. Bird.

1831

Plaintiff:	Jonathan and Gilbert
Defendant:	Duncan, Coleman; Tracy, Edward; Wahrendorff, Charles
Plaintiff's Attorney:	Bird, Gustavus A.
Defendant's Attorney:	Spalding, Josiah
Verdict:	N/A

Notes:

Petition of Jonathan and Gilbert, brothers; Gilbert was a slave owned by Coleman Duncan; Jonathan claimed he had arranged to buy Gilbert from Duncan for $400;

claimed Duncan would sell Gilbert in some "distant place" if Jonathan would not buy his brother; arranged for Jonathan to put down $100, would give Jonathan a bill of sale for Gilbert, Jonathan would emancipate Gilbert, and both brothers could pay the remaining $300 over a period of 30 months; petitioning because Gilbert was supposedly entitled to his freedom before the deal was made; requesting remaining bond for $300 held by defendants to be cancelled; included copy of bill of sale, deed of emancipation, and $300 bond; answer from defendants Tracy and Wahrendorff claiming Jonathan was aware of Gilbert's entitlement to freedom, but chose to purchase Gilbert to avoid costs and delay from a suit.

1831

Plaintiff:	Jack
Defendant:	Collins, Charles
Plaintiff's Attorney:	Stother, George F.
Defendant's Attorney:	N/A
Verdict:	N/A
Notes:	

Plaintiff claimed born in Africa; brought to South Carolina where David Williamson obtained him; from South Carolina, Williamson brought plaintiff to St. Louis; sold to Charles Collins; sold to one English, who took plaintiff to Carolton, Illinois; resided in Illinois twelve months; brought back to St. Louis by Collins where now held as a slave; William Sewel, although not mentioned in petition, impleaded as a defendant as well as Collins.

1831

Plaintiff:	Mariquette
Defendant:	McKenney, Samuel T.
Plaintiff's Attorney:	Stother, George F.
Defendant's Attorney:	Spalding, Josiah
Verdict:	Not freed
Notes:	

Plaintiff born in Kaskaskia, Illinois; about thirty-one years old; claimed sold when an infant, bought by one named Marshall; taken to Ste. Genevieve; bought six to seven months prior to the suit by Samuel McKenney; Charles Wehrendorff impleaded as a defendant as well.

1831

Plaintiff:	Richards, Nelly
Defendant:	Sewel, William
Plaintiff's Attorney:	Stother, George F.
Defendant's Attorney:	N/A
Verdict:	N/A

Notes:

Plaintiff twenty-four years old; born in Charles County, Maryland, the slave of Kitty Middleton; lived in Maryland until age fourteen; claimed "left free" upon Middleton's death; Kitty's daughter, married to William Sewel, moved plaintiff to Forquier County, Virginia, to live with Sewel family; Sewel moved to Indianapolis, Indiana, where plaintiff "allowed freedom by the judgement of the court"; Sewel then moved plaintiff to Louisville, Kentucky, and then St. Louis; now held in St. Louis as a slave; sheriff noted defendant not found in his county.

1831

Plaintiff:	Anna
Defendant:	Higginbotham, Thomas
Plaintiff's Attorney:	Bird, Gustavus A.
Defendant's Attorney:	Strother, George F.
Verdict:	Not freed

Notes:

Plaintiff claimed by defendant, but held in possession of Pleasant M. Rose of St. Louis; claimed defendant's son-in-law, John Parkinson, took plaintiff to live in Illinois as a permanent place of residence; six months prior to her suit, plaintiff was taken back to St. Louis; believed defendant intended to sell her to someone who would take her to New Orleans or "some distant place" to prevent her suing for freedom; also believed she had been given to defendant's daughter and lived in Illinois with defendant's knowledge; requested writ of habeas corpus.

1831

Plaintiff:	Louisa
Defendant:	Calvert, Sanford
Plaintiff's Attorney:	Strother, George F.
Defendant's Attorney:	Bates, Edward; Allen, Beverly
Verdict:	Not freed

Notes:

Plaintiff age nine; sued by next friend and former owner Silas L. Duval; born in Virginia; given by Duval to Sanford Calvert upon Calvert marrying Duval's daughter; Calvert took plaintiff to Galena, Illinois; kept there about two years when took her to St. Louis.

1832

Plaintiff:	Vina
Defendant:	Mitchell, Martin
Plaintiff's Attorney:	Strother, George F.; Bird, Gustavus A.
Defendant's Attorney:	Foreman, Stephen W. (attorney for Henry G. Mitchell and Henry C. Rupel)
Verdict:	Freed

Notes:

Plaintiff claimed brought to Missouri seven years earlier, by a man named Mitchell; taken to Illinois where she obtained her freedom; lived for several years as free person in both Missouri and Illinois; had lived in St. Louis since 1827; then siezed by an agent of defendant, P. Walsh, and put in jail as a runaway slave; included document that impleaded Henry G. Mitchell and Henry C. Russel into her suit.

1832

Plaintiff:	Washington, Tenor
Defendant:	Scott, Henry; Scott, John; Johnson, Jermiah
Plaintiff's Attorney:	Strother, George F.
Defendant's Attorney:	Bent, John
Verdict:	Freed

Notes:

Plaintiff born in Virginia; brought to St. Louis two years earlier by Case M. Gill; sold by Gill to defendant Henry Scott; taken by defendant Johnson to Lebanon, Illinois, with Scott's permission; lived in Illinois about twelve months; brought back to St. Louis County by Johnson; claimed by defendant John Scott, Henry's brother.

1832

Plaintiff:	John
Defendant:	Campbell, William
Plaintiff's Attorney:	Foreman, Stephen W.

Defendant's Attorney:	Spalding, Josiah
Verdict:	Freed
Notes:	

Plaintiff sued by next friend Margarett or Marguerite Sarpee; claimed mother Susett or Susan was born in Ste. Genevieve; taken to Illinois where plaintiff was born; taken short time after his birth to Missouri with his mother for about one year; taken to Galena, Illinois, where he was sold; remained in Galena until brought to St. Louis a few days before filing his suit; now held by William Campbell, who was on his way to Washington City; possible will be taken to New Orleans to be sold; included writ of habeas corpus; deposition of Francis Jarot claimed Susett and John owned by his father; claimed John not thought to be a slave past twenty-one and that Campbell had knowledge of the fact.

1832

Plaintiff:	Thenia
Defendant:	Crowder, Green
Plaintiff's Attorney:	Bates, Edward; Allen, Beverly
Defendant's Attorney:	Gamble, Hamilton R.
Verdict:	N/A
Notes:	

Petition of plaintiff, age twenty-one, and daughter Charlotte, age three; claimed born a slave in Kentucky, owner named Bozier; given to Jacob Weaver upon his marriage to Bozier's daughter; plaintiff was a "little girl" upon transfer to Weaver; remained in Kentucky until four or five years earlier when Weaver moved to Waggoner's Point, Illinois; after one year, moved across the Mississippi River to "half breed country," where Charlotte was born; Mrs. Weaver prevented plaintiff and Charlotte from being sold, upon her death, Jacob took them to St. Louis, sold to Green Crowder, a slave trader; believed would be sold soon to a "Southern market."

1832

Plaintiff:	Duncan, Coleman
Defendant:	Duncan, Jonathan
Plaintiff's Attorney:	Spalding, Josiah
Defendant's Attorney:	Gamble, Hamilton R.; Bird, Gustavus A.
Verdict:	N/A
Notes:	

Plaintiff sued to the use of James S. Thomas; claimed defendant Jonathan failed to pay bond of $300, spread out over 30 month period of $100 every 10 months, with 6 percent interest owed on last 20 months; claimed 20 months had elapsed without any payment from Jonathan; part of original agreement for Jonathan to purchase his brother Gabriel from Coleman Duncan; Jonathan claimed the original agreement was fraudulent and an act of misrepresentation as Gabriel was already entitled to his freedom; Jonathan demanded $100 he had already paid as down payment for Gabriel.

1832

Plaintiff:	Charlotte
Defendant:	Crowder, Green
Plaintiff's Attorney:	Bates, Edward; Allen, Beverly
Defendant's Attorney:	Gamble, Hamilton R.
Verdict:	Not freed
Notes:	

Plaintiff filed plea of trespass against defendant by next friend Edward Bates; included copy of order allowing plaintiff and her mother, Thenia, alias Sarah, to sue for freedom; sought $100 damages.

1832

Plaintiff:	Susan
Defendant:	Parker, Lemon
Plaintiff's Attorney:	Foreman, Stephen W.
Defendant's Attorney:	Gamble, Hamilton R.
Verdict:	Not freed
Notes:	

Plaintiff about fourteen years old; claimed born free in Kaskaskia, Illinois; her mother Dunky was enslaved at the time, owned by William Morrison; Dunky was a native African; after Morrison's daughter married Andrew Hay, plaintiff given to Hay and family; Hay sent plaintiff to Galena and sold her to defendant; defendant brought her to St. Louis; defendant's name also spelled Leman.

1832

Plaintiff:	Michael
Defendant:	Mitchell, Elijah

Plaintiff's Attorney:	Strother, George F.
Defendant's Attorney:	N/A
Verdict:	N/A

Notes:

Petition of Michael and Anson, brothers, by next friend William Clark; claimed mother, Matilda, had obtained her freedom thirteen years earlier by a judgement of the territorial government in Missouri; she moved to Illinois afterwards, where Michael and Anson were born; lived free until defendant claimed them as his slaves and "forcibly" removed them to Missouri; believed defendant and one named Russel would soon take them out of the state; included writ of habeas corpus for Michael; plea of trespass by Michael.

1832

Plaintiff:	Anson
Defendant:	Mitchell, Elijah
Plaintiff's Attorney:	Strother, George F.
Defendant's Attorney:	N/A
Verdict:	N/A

Notes:

Plaintiff filed plea of trespass against defendant by next friend William Clark; judge's orders mentioned petition from brother Michael's suit.

1832

Plaintiff:	Sam
Defendant:	Field, Alexander P; Mitchell, Elijah
Plaintiff's Attorney:	Geyer, Henry S.
Defendant's Attorney:	Foreman, Stephen W.
Verdict:	Not freed

Notes:

Plaintiff sued by mother and next friend Lydia Titus; claimed Lydia, as a slave of Elisha Mitchel, now deceased, had been taken to the territory of Illinois in 1807; after Elisha's death, sued widow and administrator of his estate, Jenny Mitchell, for her freedom; won her freedom and plaintiff was born afterwards; lived free up until the day before the filing of suit; taken as slaves by Alexander P. Field, Elijah Mitchell, and others to St. Louis; planned to immediately move plaintiff outside jurisdiction of court; included writ of habeas corpus; judge's order for plaintiff to be hired out.

1832

Plaintiff:	Nathan
Defendant:	Field, Alexander P.
Plaintiff's Attorney:	Geyer, Henry S.
Defendant's Attorney:	Foreman, Stephen W.
Verdict:	Not freed
Notes:	

Plaintiff sued by mother and next friend Lydia Titus; claimed Lydia, as a slave of Elisha Mitchell, now deceased, had been taken to the territory of Illinois, St. Clair County, in 1807; after Elisha's death, sued widow and administrator of his estate, Jenny Mitchell, for her freedom; won her freedom and plaintiff was born afterwards; lived free up until the day before the filing of suit; taken as slaves "on the road to Herculaneum" by Alexander P. Field, Elijah Mitchell, and others to St. Louis; planned to immediately move plaintiff outside jurisdiction of court; included writ of habeas corpus; judge's order for plaintiff to be hired out.

1832

Plaintiff:	Mary Ann
Defendant:	Field, Alexander P.; Mitchell, Elijah
Plaintiff's Attorney:	Geyer, Henry S.; Strother, George F.; Bird, Gustavus A.
Defendant's Attorney:	Foreman, Stephen W.
Verdict:	Freed
Notes:	

Plaintiff's name also spelled Marianne; sued by mother and next friend Lydia Titus; claimed Lydia, as a slave of Elisha Mitchell, now deceased, had been taken to the territory of Illinois in 1807; after Elisha's death, sued widow and administrator of his estate, Jenny Mitchell, for her freedom; won her freedom and plaintiff was born afterwards; lived free up until the day before the of filing suit; taken as slaves by Alexander P. Field and Elijah Mitchell to St. Louis; planned to immediately move plaintiff outside jurisdiction of court; included writ of habeas corpus; judge's order for plaintiff to be hired out; group deposition from Illinois mentioned Elisha Mitchell's slaves Bob, Lydia, Hester, Matilda, and Vina; exception to deposition by plaintiff, Vina, Mahalia, Sam, and Nathan; agreement for same verdict in cases of Mahala, Anson, Michal, and Vina.

1832

Plaintiff:	Matilda
Defendant:	Mitchell, Elijah
Plaintiff's Attorney:	Strother, George F.
Defendant's Attorney:	N/A
Verdict:	Freed

Notes:

Plaintiff claimed to have obtained her freedom thirteen years earlier by a judgement of the territorial government in Missouri; had lived since that time in Illinois; kidnapped from Illinois May 1832 and held as slave by defendant; believed would be taken out of the jurisdiction of the court soon.

1832

Plaintiff:	Matilda
Defendant:	Mitchell, Henry G.; Russell, Henry
Plaintiff's Attorney:	Strother, George F.
Defendant's Attorney:	Foreman, Stephen W.
Verdict:	Freed

Notes:

Included plea of trespass against defendants; judge's order to hire plaintiff out; writ of habeas corpus with sherriff's note that plaintiff was held in jail at Jefferson City for her "personal safety"; plea of not guilty by defendants.

1832

Plaintiff:	Michael
Defendant:	Mitchell, Henry G.; Russell, Henry
Plaintiff's Attorney:	Strother, George F.
Defendant's Attorney:	Foreman, Stephen W.
Verdict:	Freed

Notes:

Included plea of trespass against defendants; judge's order to hire plaintiff out; writ of habeas corpus; plea of not guilty by defendants; plaintiff sued by next friend William Clark.

1832

Plaintiff:	Anson
Defendant:	Mitchell, Henry; Russell, Henry
Plaintiff's Attorney:	Strother, George F.
Defendant's Attorney:	Foreman, Stephen W.
Verdict:	Freed
Notes:	

Included plea of trespass against defendants; judge's order to hire plaintiff out; writ of habeas corpus with sherriff's note that plaintiff was held in jail at Jefferson City for him "personal safety"; note also mentioned defendants had been arrested on charges of kidnapping; Mitchell arrested under name "Martin"; plea of not guilty by defendants.

1832

Plaintiff:	Washington, Tenor
Defendant:	Scott, Henry; Emerson, John
Plaintiff's Attorney:	Magenis, Arthur L.
Defendant's Attorney:	N/A
Verdict:	N/A
Notes:	

Plaintiff born a slave; belonged to Cajabal Gill who sold him to Jeremiah Johnston in 1830; Johnston took him to Lebanon, Illinois, for one year; transferred him to defendant; taken to St. Louis by defendant; included affadavit from William Mull asking for revocation of nonsuit, stating he was aiding plaintiff's suit and had been away on business on the trial date; had located Gill in Carollton, Illinois, and could get his testimony for the witness; stated defendant said he would send plaintiff "down the river" before she could file another suit against him; John Emerson impleaded with Scott in plea of trespass.

1832

Plaintiff:	Leah
Defendant:	Mitchell, Arthur
Plaintiff's Attorney:	Bird, Gustavus A.
Defendant's Attorney:	Newman, John
Verdict:	Not freed
Notes:	

Plaintiff's name also spelled Lea; sued for herself, but claimed her two children's right to freedom within suit, Archibald and Brunetta; claimed defendant moved her from Kentucky to Ohio in 1817; plaintiff brought suit against defendant at the Brown County, Ohio, Court of Common Pleas in April of 1826; court ruled for her freedom; held as a slave by defendant in St. Louis, but about to be sold out of the jurisdiction of the court; claimed kept $700 of her wages; included $1,000 recognizance bond for Leah, Archibald, and Brunetta.

1832

Plaintiff:	Mahala
Defendant:	Mitchell, Martin
Plaintiff's Attorney:	Bird, Gustavus A.
Defendant's Attorney:	Foreman, Stephen W.
Verdict:	Not freed
Notes:	

Plaintif sued by next friend Gustavaus A. Bird; claimed born free in Illinois in 1812; mother was free at her birth, and "been regarded . . . as free" by everyone who knew her; Lydia's former owner, Elisha Mitchell, deceased, had brought her into Illinois from Kentucky; hired her out for three months; stated Elisha had intended for Lydia to be free; recently arrested as a runaway slave, and claimed by defendant as the attorney "in fact" for Elijah Mitchell, deceased; believed defendant intended to take her to Kentucky, and had already attempted to place her on board the steamboat *Union*; deposition of Ichabod Badgley to be used in the cases of Vina, Sam, Anson, Marianne, Matilda, and Michael; included notice to take deposition for plaintiff, Matilda, Vina, Sam, Nathan, Marianne, Anson, and Michael; Badgley's deposition named Nase Titus as Lydia's husband in Illinois; also mentioned Elisha's slaves Lyd, Duck, Sam, Mahala, Matilda, Vina, and Bob; included writ of habeas corpus.

1833

Plaintiff:	Harriet
Defendant:	McKenney, Samuel T.; Walker, William; James, Thomas D.
Plaintiff's Attorney:	Bird, Gustavus A.
Defendant's Attorney:	N/A
Verdict:	Freed
Notes:	

Plaintiff under the age of twenty-one; sued by mother Julia, and next friend Gustavus A. Bird; claimed in October 1829, then owner Lucinda Carrington took plaintiff and mother from Kentucky to settle in Pike County, Illinois; kept them there about three months until "it became a talk" among neighbors that plaintiff and her mother were free; Carrington sent plaintiff and her mother to Missouri where hired them out for nine months; came back to Illinois for eight weeks; sent back to Missouri, where sold to Samuel McKenney; held by McKenney or Thomas D. James, a slave trader in St. Louis.

1833

Plaintiff:	Ralph
Defendant:	Duncan, Robert; Duncan, James
Plaintiff's Attorney:	Bird, Gustavus A.
Defendant's Attorney:	Geyer, Henry S.; Bates, Edward
Verdict:	N/A

Notes:

Plaintiff also known as Ralph Gordon; filed plea of trespass against defendants; claimed they kept $500 of his wages illegally; included special verdict and judgement that identified plaintiff as previously suing Coleman Duncan; defendants had entered into recognizance to hire out plaintiff; disputed wages were those earned during period of hire; included details of the hire, naming David Lawrence as a employer or renter of plaintiff; included appeal by plaintiff.

1833

Plaintiff:	Harriet
Defendant:	McKenney
Plaintiff's Attorney:	Bird, Gustavus A.
Defendant's Attorney:	Gamble, Hamilton R.
Verdict:	Freed

Notes:

Plaintiff under the age of twenty-one; filed plea of trespass by next friend Gustavus A. Bird; record book page reference on McKenney's plea noted McKenney died and Lucinda Carrington, plaintiff's former owner, stepped in as defendant; included defendant's exception to depositions of Nancy Bright and William Scholle.

1833

Plaintiff:	Sarah
Defendant:	Johnson, Thomas; Johnson, Janus
Plaintiff's Attorney:	Strother, George F.
Defendant's Attorney:	N/A
Verdict:	Not freed
Notes:	

Plaintiff under the age of twenty-one; sued by next friend Isham Williams; claimed born free in Jefferson County, Missouri; brought to St. Louis by Johnson and claimed as his slave; was trying and had already tried to sell her to Janus [possibly Thomas D. James], a slave trader in St. Louis; feared was to be sold in Mississippi or Louisiana, out of the jurisdiction of the court.

1833

Plaintiff:	Wilkinson, James
Defendant:	Young, Aaron
Plaintiff's Attorney:	Bird, Gustavus A.
Defendant's Attorney:	N/A
Verdict:	Freed
Notes:	

Plaintiff claimed came to an agreement with defendant to purchase his freedom; was to pay $200 to Young, who would liberate him to work and pay off remainder; did pay Young $200 in 1827 and since paid off remainder over four years earlier; Young still claimed and held petitioner as a slave in St. Louis; mentioned working with Young's permission for Osborn in Illinois for four months, as well as Young's brother, a doctor in Galena, Illinois, for four months.

1833

Plaintiff:	Mary
Defendant:	Menard, Francis; Busby, Daniel
Plaintiff's Attorney:	Darby, John F.
Defendant's Attorney:	N/A
Verdict:	Freed
Notes:	

Plaintiff's petition listed all activity on her suit since originally filed petition July 31, 1827; was twenty-six or twenty-seven at time of original filing; original petition stated she was born in Kaskaskia, Illinois, into the family and ownership of Michel Bivenue; upon Bivenue's death, sold to Francis Menard who sent her to St. Louis to be hired out three years prior to her petition; was hired out to Andre Landreville, whom she brought her original suit against along with Menard; Landreville denied ownership and Menard stayed out of jurisdiction of court, avoiding trial; as suit continued, Menard evaded trial until her previous attorneys, Issac C. McGirk and John N. Bass, either died or "left the states"; her original suit abated for want to someone to present it; she and her eldest daughter Virginia, age thirteen, had recently been siezed by Sidney Brase and Daniel Busby, acting as agents of Menard, to prevent her bringing a new suit; claimed Menard would continue to stay out of jurisdiction of court, but prayed to allow suit for herself and her children, Virginia, Victoire, age twelve, and Elizabeth, age eight.

1833

Plaintiff:	Vincent, Adolphe
Defendant:	Leduc, Marie P.
Plaintiff's Attorney:	Magenis, Arthur L.
Defendant's Attorney:	Bates, Edward
Verdict:	Freed
Notes:	

Petition for Adolphe, Marcelline, and Maria; plaintiff sued through next friend Charles St. Vrain; petition identified plaintiff, Marcelline, and Maria as the children of Louise Vincent, who was a slave in St. Louis at the time of their birth; owned by widow and heirs of Antoine Vincent Bouis, deceased; sold in 1829 at public sale to Joshua Pahlen; Pahlen took them to his residence in Illinois, keeping them there twelve to fifteen months; Pahlen died three or four months prior to their petition; claimed by Marie P. Leduc, administrator to Pahlen's estate; included Adolphe's plea of trespass; deposition from Carthage, Hancock County, Illinois.

1833

Plaintiff:	Vincent, Marcelline
Defendant:	Leduc, Marie P.
Plaintiff's Attorney:	Magenis, Arthur L.

Defendant's Attorney:	Bates, Edward
Verdict:	Freed
Notes:	

Plea of trespass by plaintiff by next friend Charles St. Vrain; included copy of judge's order mentioning petition of Adolphe and Maria, siblings of plaintiffs; summons mentioned plaintiff's mother Louise Vincent; included deposition from Carthage, Hancock County, Illinois.

1833

Plaintiff:	Vincent, Louise
Defendant:	Leduc, Marie P.
Plaintiff's Attorney:	Magenis, Arthur L.
Defendant's Attorney:	Bates, Edward
Verdict:	Freed
Notes:	

Plaintiff about thirty years old; born a slave of Antoine Bouis, deceased, in St. Louis; continued to serve his widow and heirs until 1829 when sold at public sale to Joshua Pahlen (also Pahlin); Pahlen bought plaintiff and her three children, Adolphe, Marcelline, and Maria, for $750; moved them to his residence in Illinois; lived there about fifteen months; three or four months before petition filed Pahlen died; claimed by defendant, administrator to Pahlen's estate; included affidavits from Louise and her attorney Arthur L. Magenis to be considered for all the cases of Louise, Adolphe, and Marcelline; affidavits stated main witness Charles St. Vrain gave "materially varied" testimony at the trials then he had previously given; had based case on his testimony and no others; affadavit to set aside nonsuits in all three cases and request to attain additional testimonies; deposition from Carthage, Hancock County, Illinois.

1834

Plaintiff:	Reuben
Defendant:	Morrison, William; Swan, John C.
Plaintiff's Attorney:	Strother, George F.
Defendant's Attorney:	N/A
Verdict:	Not freed
Notes:	

Plaintiff also called Reuben Morrison; about thirty-five years old; claimed born in

South Carolina; taken by Robert Morrison to Illinois about twenty-one years before filing his suit; later claimed by William Morrison in Illinois; taken into Missouri for about nine months; taken back into Illinois and into Michigan Territory for four years; Morrison brought plaintiff back to Illinois and placed him in the possession of John Swan, the captain of the steamboat *Missouri*; afterwards in possession of one named Willis; at time of petition, again in the possession of Swan.

1834

Plaintiff:	Henry
Defendant:	Morrison, William; Swan, John C.
Plaintiff's Attorney:	Strother, George F.
Defendant's Attorney:	N/A
Verdict:	Not freed
Notes:	

Plaintiff also called Henry Morrison; about twenty-one years old; claimed born in St. Clair, Illinois; owned by William Morrison who took plaintiff to Michigan Territory about seven or eight years earlier; after four years, Morrison returned with plaintiff to Illinois; placed in the possession of John Swan, captain of the *Missouri*; Swan gave plaintiff to one called Willis in New Orleans; two weeks later repossessed by Swan.

1834

Plaintiff:	Dutton, Lemmon
Defendant:	Paca, John
Plaintiff's Attorney:	Gamble, Hamilton R.
Defendant's Attorney:	Bates, Edward
Verdict:	Freed
Notes:	

Plaintiff sued by mother and next friend Grace, a free woman of color; claimed that in 1787, grandmother, Hannah, given deed of emancipation by her owner Josias William Dallam, she was to be emancipated in thirteen years; Dallam also entered the condition that Hannah's children and grandchildren "born into slavery" would receive their freedom upon reaching age twenty-three; Grace was born to Hannah in 1792; Hannah gave birth to plaintiff in 1816, after passing the age of twenty-three; plaintiff, however, was held in slavery by defendant, the son-in-law to Dallam; included bill of exceptions from 1836; included agreement that Lemmon's suit would be appealed to Missouri Supreme Court, and the suits of Andrew and Abraham would follow same decision; transcript of Missouri Supreme Court Justice Mathias McGirk's opinion; transcript of 1787 deed of emancipation; mentioned Dallam's slaves Marlborough, Orange, Lemon, Nance, Hannah, and Sook.

1834

Plaintiff:	Dutton, Andrew
Defendant:	Paca, John
Plaintiff's Attorney:	Gamble, Hamilton R.
Defendant's Attorney:	Bates, Edward
Verdict:	Freed

Notes:

Plaintiff sued by mother and next friend Grace, a free woman of color; claimed that in 1787, grandmother, Hannah, given deed of emancipation by her owner Josias William Dallam, she was to be emancipated in thirteen years; Dallam also entered the condition that Hannah's children and grandchildren "born into slavery" would receive their freedom upon reaching age twenty-three; Grace was born to Hannah in 1792; Hannah gave birth to plaintiff in 1818, after passing the age of twenty-three; plaintiff, however, was held in slavery by defendant, the son-in-law to Dallam; included bill of exceptions from 1836.

1834

Plaintiff:	Abraham, Dutton
Defendant:	Paca, John
Plaintiff's Attorney:	Gamble, Hamilton R.
Defendant's Attorney:	Bates, Edward
Verdict:	Freed

Notes:

Plaintiff sued by mother and next friend Grace, a free woman of color; claimed that in 1787, grandmother, Hannah, given deed of emancipation by her owner Josias William Dallam, she was to be emancipated in thirteen years; Dallam also entered the condition that Hannah's children and grandchildren "born into slavery" would receive their freedom upon reaching age twenty-three; Grace was born to Hannah in 1792; Hannah gave birth to plaintiff in 1819, after passing the age of twenty-three; plaintiff, however, was held in slavery by defendant, the son-in-law to Dallam; included bill of exceptions from 1836.

1834

Plaintiff:	Kerr, Nelson
Defendant:	Kerr, Matthew
Plaintiff's Attorney:	Bird, Gustavus A.
Defendant's Attorney:	Gamble, Hamilton R.
Verdict:	Not freed
Notes:	

Plaintiff held by defendant in St. Louis; claimed that in the months of September, October, November, and December of 1833, and January and February of 1834, defendant hired plaintiff out to a Mr. Adams in Illinois; all wages for his work were paid to defendant; claimed damages of $500.

1834

Plaintiff:	Henry, James
Defendant:	Walker, William
Plaintiff's Attorney:	Spalding, Josiah
Defendant's Attorney:	Gamble, Hamilton R.
Verdict:	Freed
Notes:	

Plaintiff filed plea of trespass by next friend Josiah Spalding; copy of judge's order stated plaintiff was Rachel's son; included bill of exceptions; mentioned Fort Snelling; plaintiff born at Prarie du Chien.

1834

Plaintiff:	Mary Ann
Defendant:	Duncan, Robert
Plaintiff's Attorney:	Bird, Gustavus, A.
Defendant's Attorney:	Sproat, Harris L.
Verdict:	Freed
Notes:	

Plaintiff, alias Julia, sued by next friend James Lasser; claimed born free; mother born free in Pennsylvania, but indentured until age twenty-eight; originally indentured to Mr. Page, who sold her service to Zumer; service again sold to John L. Dutton; plaintiff had been born in St. Louis and had been claimed as a slave by Dutton since her birth; claimed by Duncan as well; her mother had been sold away to Louisiana in 1820 to prevent her gaining her freedom; plaintiff feared sale as well; testimony of Lasser named plaintiff's mother as Tillis.

1834

Plaintiff:	Rachel
Defendant:	Walker, William
Plaintiff's Attorney:	Spalding, Josiah
Defendant's Attorney:	Gamble, Hamilton R.
Verdict:	Not freed

Notes:

Plaintiff twenty years old; was previously owned by T.B.W. Stockton; taken to Prairie du Chien of Michigan Territory for two years; son James Henry was born while plaintiff lived with Stockton and his family there; Stockton later brought plaintiff and her son to St. Louis; sold them to Joseph Klunk, who sold them to William Walker, a slave trader; plaintiff believed Walker would transport her downriver, "probably New Orleans" and sell both her and son; included bill of exceptions that noted testimony of E. J. Langham and Josiah Spalding; included Missouri Supreme Court opinion by justice Mathias McGirk; cited *Winney v. Whitesides, LaGrange v. Menard,* and *Julia v. McKinney* in the issue of the Ordinance of 1787; discussed the legality of an officer of the military holding slaves in free territory.

1835

Plaintiff:	Lewis
Defendant:	Newton, James; Cooper, Jacob
Plaintiff's Attorney:	Bird, Gustavus A.
Defendant's Attorney:	Drake, Charles D.
Verdict:	Freed

Notes:

Plaintiff claimed owned by Benjamin Duncan in Kentucky; in fall of 1822, removed with his brother Ben and several other of Duncan's slaves to Indiana; hired out at Troy, Indiana for about six weeks; taken back to Kentucky and sold to John Newton; taken to St. Louis by Newton and hired out to Jacob Cooper; Newton still resided in Kentucky; claimed Cooper trying to sell him as a slave; believed Newton sent to St. Louis to prevent plaintiff from suing for his freedom and now threatened to send out of state to prevent the same; claimed two of Duncan's slaves had already gotten their freedom; included affidavits for a continuance from Gustavus A. Bird and plaintiff; depositions mentioned slaves of Duncan: Moses, Lewis, Ben, and Judy along with twenty-one unnamed others.

1835

Plaintiff:	Ligon, Nancy
Defendant:	Ligon, Daniel; Myers, William
Plaintiff's Attorney:	Bird, Gustavus A.
Defendant's Attorney:	N/A
Verdict:	N/A
Notes:	

Plaintiff claimed in summer of 1833, owner Daniel Ligon took her to his residence in Galena, Illinois, and held her as a slave; Ligon kept plaintiff in Illinois for a year or more; further claimed held by William Myers, who pretended to be an agent of Daniel Ligon.

1835

Plaintiff:	Judy (Julia Logan)
Defendant:	Meachum, John Berry
Plaintiff's Attorney:	Bird, Gustavus A.
Defendant's Attorney:	Drake, Charles D.
Verdict:	N/A
Notes:	

Plaintiff claimed approximately ten years before the filing of her petition, previous owner, Benjamin Duncan of Kentucky, hired her out in Indiana for one month; brought plaintiff back to Kentucky, sent her to Missouri, and sold her to defendant; defendant allowed plaintiff to hire herself out for twelve dollars a month; hired herself out in Galena, Illinois, for one month; plaintiff feared defendant would sell her to "some distant place"; petition included testimony of Lewis Duncan, "a man of color"; included affidavit from Charles D. Drake asking for new trial, objecting to the allowance of Lewis Duncan's testimony when a white man, James Newton, was included in the case; included bill of exceptions, which cited Edmund Jennings as plaintiff's employer in Indiana and James Newton as owner before Meachum; jury instructions; defense for Lewis as a witness.

1835

Plaintiff:	Hetty
Defendant:	Magenis, Arthur L.
Plaintiff's Attorney:	Gamble, Hamilton R.
Defendant's Attorney:	Magenis, Arthur L.

Verdict: N/A

Notes:

Plaintiff claimed born a slave in Virginia; owned by John Relf, who died in Virginia; Relf's widow, Jane, took plaintiff to Ste. Genevieve County, Missouri, in December of 1833; kept there one month before moved to Illinois, ten miles outside Kaskaskia; plaintiff lived with mistress and her son Dr. James H. Relf approximately two months before sent back to Ste. Genevieve to work; returned to the Relfs in Illinois September of 1817; lived in Illinois as a slave until July of 1818 when sent again to Ste. Genevieve with Elizabeth Linn, Jane's daughter; at time of petition in the possession of defendant in St. Louis; included affadavit from defendant to "quash" suit.

1835

Plaintiff: Steel, Mary Ann
Defendant: Skinner, Curtis
Plaintiff's Attorney: Bird, Gustavus A.
Defendant's Attorney: Spalding, Josiah
Verdict: N/A

Notes:

Plaintiff, under the age of twenty-one, filed plea of trespass by next friend Gustavus A. Bird; claimed defendant detained her as a runaway for ten days; kept her from earning $200 while imprisoned; defendant claimed plaintiff was born a slave and had always been treated a slave; claimed he had no knowledge of her entitlement to freedom; claimed plaintiff was sold and delivered to him as a slave for life.

1835

Plaintiff: Melvin, Sally
Defendant: Cohen, Robert
Plaintiff's Attorney: Bird, Gustavus A.
Defendant's Attorney: Spalding, Josiah
Verdict: N/A

Notes:

Plaintiff filed plea of trespass against defendant; claimed $500 damages; included defendant's plea against plaintiff's charges.

1835

Plaintiff:	Wilson, Daniel
Defendant:	Cohen, Robert
Plaintiff's Attorney:	Bird, Gustavus A.
Defendant's Attorney:	N/A
Verdict:	N/A
Notes:	

Plaintiff filed plea of trespass against defendant; claimed $500 damages.

1835

Plaintiff:	Steel, Mary
Defendant:	Walker, William
Plaintiff's Attorney:	Bird, Gustavus A.
Defendant's Attorney:	Spalding, Josiah
Verdict:	N/A
Notes:	

Plaintiff about sixteen years old; claimed in 1821, her former owner, Catherine Steel of Kentucky, had written into her will that plaintiff and her mother should be emancipated upon her death; Catherine had acquired plaintiff after the death of James Steel; after Catherine's death, the heirs of James Steel claimed the emancipation was invalid; they planned to sell plaintiff and her mother, and divide the proceeds among them; Charles Landers took the matter to court, and Catherine's will was upheld as legitimate; although emancipated, plaintiff agreed to continue residing with Rosanna and Greenberry Steel until she turned eighteen "to pay for her raising"; Greenberry took plaintiff, three years before the filing of the suit, to Missouri and sold her as a slave until the 25th day of July 1840; sold to Curtis Skinner who sold her to William Walker with the same condition.

1835

Plaintiff:	Wilson, Daniel
Defendant:	Melvin, Edmund
Plaintiff's Attorney:	Bird, Gustavus A.; Sproat, Harris L.
Defendant's Attorney:	Spalding, Josiah
Verdict:	Freed
Notes:	

Plaintiff claimed owner Edmond Mellvin, also spelled Melvin, settled permanently in Illinois keeping plaintiff as a slave; hired Plaintif out for two weeks in Lebanon; plaintiff then sent to Missouri; in July of 1834 sent back to Illinois where hired out again for two weeks; again sent back to Missouri where held in slavery by defendant; included bill of exception which mentioned testimony of John Atchinson, a school teacher; appeal for a new trial to Supreme Court.

1835

Plaintiff:	Johnson, Mary (Bevinue)
Defendant:	Menard, Michael
Plaintiff's Attorney:	Mayfield, James C.; Bowlin, James B.
Defendant's Attorney:	Bogg, Lewis V.
Verdict:	Not freed
Notes:	

Plaintiff about thirty-two years old; claimed born in Kaskaskia, Illinois; owned by Michael Bevinue, deceased; alleged Benivue manumitted her with all his other slaves and servants in his will; had been living free past twelve months in St. Louis until claimed by defendant as a slave.

1835

Plaintiff:	Tyler, Eliza
Defendant:	Campbell, Nelson
Plaintiff's Attorney:	Darby, John F.
Defendant's Attorney:	Learned, [Charles J.]; Hamilton, [William S. or Alexander]
Verdict:	Freed
Notes:	

Plaintiff about age twenty-three; claimed born a slave in Virginia; brought by her master to St. Louis; owned by the Cheek family; sold to George Taylor who resided in Galena, Illinois; lived in Galena until April of 1835 when visited St. Louis with consent of Taylor; sold by Taylor in Galena to Perry Burk, also a resident of Galena; sold by William Hempstead, an agent of Burk, to defendant, a slave trader from Louisiana or Mississippi; believed would soon be moved to the "lower country" to be sold.

1835

Plaintiff:	Farnham, Mary
Defendant:	Walker, Samuel D.
Plaintiff's Attorney:	Darby, John F.
Defendant's Attorney:	N/A
Verdict:	N/A
Notes:	

Plaintiff about twenty-one or twenty-two years old; claimed born a slave in Ste. Genevieve, Missouri; held by the family of John B. Bussier until 1830; brought to St. Louis and sold to Russel Farnham; taken by Farnham to Fort Edwards in Illinois, located at the lower rapids of the Mississippi River; kept in Illinois for about a year; brought back to St. Louis where Farnham died; sold by Pierre Chouteau Jr., as administrator to Farnham's estate, to defendant; claimed defendant was a resident of Louisiana.

1835

Plaintiff:	Sally
Defendant:	Chouteau, Henry
Plaintiff's Attorney:	Primm, Wilson; Drake, Charles D.
Defendant's Attorney:	Allen, Beverly
Verdict:	Freed
Notes:	

Plaintiff, age thirteen, sued by next friend Samuel Willi; claimed that mother Marianne, and her children, were freed by agreement between Marie Therese Brazeau, the widow of Joseph Brazeau, deceased, and Baptiste Duchouquette and Marie Therese his wife, the niece of Joseph Brazeau; however, after the death of Joseph's wife and his niece, plaintiff, daughter of Marianne, was sold by the heirs of Brazeau and Duchouquette; plaintiff sold in St. Louis to defendant; petition included excerpt from written agreement; also mentioned slaves Bob, who was also to be freed, and Baptiste who would be willed to future heirs; included bill of exceptions.

1835

Plaintiff:	Milly
Defendant:	Duncan, James
Plaintiff's Attorney:	Polk, Trusten; Gamble, Hamilton R.
Defendant's Attorney:	N/A

Verdict: Not freed

Notes:

Plaintiff born a slave in Kentucky, the property of Jesse Duncan; came into owner-ship of defendant; July 1834, defendant took plaintiff to Galena, Illinois, holding her there three to four weeks; then took plaintiff to "Dubuques," on the western side of the Mississippi River and north of Missouri; plaintiff worked from August or September 1834 till June 1835 in the mines there; after attempting to bring suit for freedom in Dubuques, plaintiff moved to Louisiana, Missouri, and St. Louis; note from sheriff stating defendant not found.

1835

Plaintiff:	LaCourse, Josephine
Defendant:	Mitchell, George
Plaintiff's Attorney:	Magenis, Arthur L.
Defendant's Attorney:	Bates, Edward
Verdict:	Not freed

Notes:

Plaintiff sued by mother and next friend Julia La Course; claimed born in French Village, St. Clair County, Illinois, in 1826; claimed by Baptishe La Course as a slave; sold to Charles Bone, also a resident of Illinois; sold to Edward Mitchell, who brought plaintiff to St. Louis; affidavit from Arthur L. Magenis claiming plaintiff had been removed out of the jurisdiction of the court by either by defendant or James Mitchell, father of defendant, or both; requested attachment of contempt of court against defendant; included statement of defendant claiming he had been in Kentucky at time of removal of plaintiff; claimed plaintiff had always belonged to his father and had only borrowed her to temporarily serve his wife.

1835

Plaintiff:	Agnis (Agathe)
Defendant:	Menard, Pierre
Plaintiff's Attorney:	Mayfield, James J.; Bowlin, James B.
Defendant's Attorney:	Allen, Beverly
Verdict:	N/A

Notes:

Plaintiff about twenty-two years old; claimed born in Kaskaskia, Illinois; mother an indentured servant or slave; believed that plaintiff was never indentured or registered as an indentured servant; left Illinois four years earlier, moved to St. Louis; a few days before filing of suit, defendant had claimed her as his slave; defendant about to move her out of the state, causing plaintiff to "lose all evidence of her freedom"; included petition from defendant for a change of venue; bond by Beverly Allen to guarantee Menard's appearance at a different venue.

1835

Plaintiff:	Courtney
Defendant:	Rayburn, Samuel
Plaintiff's Attorney:	Drake, Charles D.; [Manning, Alonzo W.]
Defendant's Attorney:	Spalding, Josiah
Verdict:	Not freed
Notes:	

Plaintiff, age twenty-three, and infant son William sued for freedom; born in Virgina, owned by Garland, sold to his brother John Garland, U.S. Army, who took to Michigan Territory, sold to Alexis Bay in St. Peters; sold to defendant in St. Louis.

1836

Plaintiff:	Ben
Defendant:	White, Thomas J.; Woods, William L.
Plaintiff's Attorney:	Bird, Gustavus A.; Bowlin, James B.
Defendant's Attorney:	Hudson, [Thomas B.]; Hamilton, Alexander
Verdict:	Freed
Notes:	

Plaintiff held in St. Louis as slave by White for Woods of Virginia; fall and winter of 1833 brought by Granger to mine coal in St. Clair County, Illinois; hired out to Woods's brother-in-law in same county; four depositions reaffirmed employment.

1836

Plaintiff:	Logan, Green Berry
Defendant:	Meachum, John Berry
Plaintiff's Attorney:	Risque, Ferdinand W.
Defendant's Attorney:	N/A
Verdict:	Freed
Notes:	

Plaintiff, five years old, by mother Judy Logan, sued for freedom; Judy, twelve years prior, was a slave of Benjamin Duncan of Kentucky, was sent out for hire in Indiana; both sold to defendant; Judy granted freedom in previous suit; sued for Green's freedom on same grounds.

1836

Plaintiff:	Phillis
Defendant:	Herring, Redding B.
Plaintiff's Attorney:	Bird, Gustavus A.
Defendant's Attorney:	Geyer, Henry S.
Verdict:	Not freed
Notes:	

Plaintiff, a free person of color by Louisiana Supreme Court ruling; also known as Susan; alleged defendant abducted and held her in irons for twelve days in Illinois, shipped her to Louisiana where sold her as a slave in 1824; pursued damages $5,000.

1836

Plaintiff:	Delph
Defendant:	Dorris, Stephen
Plaintiff's Attorney:	Spalding, Josiah; Stone, J.
Defendant's Attorney:	Gamble, [Hamilton R.]; Allen, [Beverley]
Verdict:	Not freed
Notes:	

Plaintiff alleged she was freed upon death of former owner, Josiah Ramsey, of Kentucky before sale to defendant in St. Louis; bill of sale with other slaves names included; depositions from Kentucky for defendant also included.

1837

Plaintiff:	Aspasia
Defendant:	Rosati, Joseph
Plaintiff's Attorney:	Risque, Ferdinand W.
Defendant's Attorney:	N/A
Verdict:	Not freed
Notes:	

Also Aspisa; plaintiff's mother, Judy, held as a slave in Vincennes, Indiana, and Kaskaskia, Illinois, in Northwest territory; suit based on mother's suit for freedom; mentioned Ordinance of 1787; William LeCompte; Robert Bunton; defendant a Bishop in St. Louis.

1837

Plaintiff:	Judy
Defendant:	Meachum, John Berry
Plaintiff's Attorney:	Risque, Ferdinand W.
Defendant's Attorney:	N/A
Verdict:	Freed

Notes:

Judy, also Little Judy, born in Virginia; sold to William Sullivan of Louisville, Kentucky; sold to Robert Bunton of Vincennes, Indiana; sold to William LeCompte; held by Meachum; mentioned Pierre Menard; slaves Old Judy, William, Sarah, Louisa, Nancy, Phillis; document in French.

1837

Plaintiff:	Andrew
Defendant:	Sarpy, John B.
Plaintiff's Attorney:	Risque, Ferdinand W.
Defendant's Attorney:	Geyer, Henry S.
Verdict:	Freed

Notes:

Plaintiff, age sixteen; through grandmother Judy, sued for freedom based on Judy's suit; mentioned Louisville, Kentucky; Francis Crely; William Sullivan; Robert Bunton; Pierre Menard; Toussaint DeBois; Pierre Chouteau; Wilson Primm.

1837

Plaintiff:	Aspasia
Defendant:	Lane, Hardage
Plaintiff's Attorney:	Risque, Ferdinand W.; Bird, Gustavus
Defendant's Attorney:	Geyer, Henry S.; Hudson, Thomas B.; Primm, Wilson
Verdict:	Not freed

Notes:

Plaintiff, also Aspisa, thirty-two years old, daughter of Judy; mentioned slaves Old Judy, William, Sally, Louisa, Nancy; Judy's son Toussaint; Vincennes, Indiana; Kaskaskia, Illinois; included bill of sale in Spanish; document citing decisions in Missouri in cases for freedom.

1837

Plaintiff:	Celeste
Defendant:	Papin, Laforce
Plaintiff's Attorney:	Risque, Ferdinand W.
Defendant's Attorney:	N/A
Verdict:	Not freed

Notes:

Plaintiff, age twenty-six, daughter of Judy; suit based on mother's suit for freedom; mentioned Louisville, Kentucky; Vincennes, Indiana; Robert Bunton, Kaskaskia, Illinois; William LeCompte; Ordinance of 1787.

1837

Plaintiff:	Celestine
Defendant:	Papin, Laforce
Plaintiff's Attorney:	Risque, Ferdinand W.
Defendant's Attorney:	N/A
Verdict:	Not freed

Notes:

Plaintiff, age one, through grandmother Judy, sued for freedom based on Judy's suit; daughter of Celeste; mentioned Louisville, Kentucky; William Sullivan; Robert Bunton, Vincennes, Indiana; Kaskaskia, Illinois; Ordinance of 1787; William LeCompte.

1837

Plaintiff:	George, Lewis
Defendant:	Burd, William
Plaintiff's Attorney:	Strother, George F.; Hudson, Thomas B.
Defendant's Attorney:	Gamble, Hamilton R.
Verdict:	Freed

Notes:

Plaintiff claimed born to free parents in Campell County, Virginia; claimed defendant from same county, moved plaintiff to St. Louis and held illegally in slavery; See also St. Louis Circuit Court case 1837 July Term #133, William Stubs.

1837

Plaintiff:	Stubbs, William
Defendant:	Burd, William
Plaintiff's Attorney:	Strother, George F.; Hudson, Thomas B.
Defendant's Attorney:	Gamble, Hamilton R.
Verdict:	Freed
Notes:	

Plaintiff claimed born to free parents in Campell County, Virginia; claimed defendant from same county, moved plaintiff to St. Louis and held illegally in slavery; Includes joint petition from Lewis and William Stubs; See also St. Louis Circuit Court July Term case #132, Lewis Stubs.

1837

Plaintiff:	Jack
Defendant:	Link, Absalom
Plaintiff's Attorney:	Spalding, Josiah
Defendant's Attorney:	Magenis, Arthur L.
Verdict:	Not freed
Notes:	

Plaintiff born in Virginia, slave of Harrison Winn; Winn moved to Illinois, hired Jack out in Shawneetown; Winn sold Jack to William Thompson; Thompson sold Jack to Absalom Link in St. Louis.

1837

Plaintiff:	Stubbs, Nancy
Defendant:	Burd, William
Plaintiff's Attorney:	Hudson, Thomas B.
Defendant's Attorney:	N/A
Verdict:	Freed
Notes:	

Plaintiff alleged she was a free person; claimed the defendant unlawfully held her in slavery; sought $100 damages.

1837

Plaintiff:	Stubbs, Robert
Defendant:	Burd, William
Plaintiff's Attorney:	Hudson, Thomas B.
Defendant's Attorney:	N/A
Verdict:	Freed

Notes:

Plaintiff alleged he was a free person; claimed the defendant unlawfully held him in slavery; sought $100 damages.

1837

Plaintiff:	Stubbs, Phoebe
Defendant:	Burd, William
Plaintiff's Attorney:	Hudson, Thomas B.
Defendant's Attorney:	N/A
Verdict:	Freed

Notes:

Plaintiff alleged she was a free person; claimed the defendant unlawfully held her in slavery; sought $1,000 damages.

1838

Plaintiff:	Stokes, Samuel
Defendant:	Finney, John; Finney, William
Plaintiff's Attorney:	Bird, Gustavus A.
Defendant's Attorney:	N/A
Verdict:	N/A

Notes:

Stokes and wife, free persons of color, sued for freedom of grandchildren Mary and John; Finneys bought daughter Charity and Mary to keep until Stokes could purchase them; kept as slaves and Charity sold; Charity died in servitude; Stokes had paid $225 towards contract with Finneys.

1839

Plaintiff:	Wash, Polly
Defendant:	Magehan, Joseph M.
Plaintiff's Attorney:	Sproat, Harris L.

Defendant's Attorney:	Allen, Beverly
Verdict:	Freed
Notes:	

Plaintiff from Wayne County, Kentucky; owner Joseph Crockett; moved her to Illinois, town four miles from Edwardsville; hired out as domestic; sold to Taylor Berry; upon Berry's death, Judge Wash married widow; hired out Polly to Steamboat *Banner* as chambermaid.

1839

Plaintiff:	Aspasia (Aspisa)
Defendant:	Lane, Hardage
Plaintiff's Attorney:	Risque, Ferdinand W.
Defendant's Attorney:	Hudson, Thomas B.; Geyer, Henry S.
Verdict:	N/A
Notes:	

Plaintiff, a free woman of color, claimed $800 damages for being held by defendant as slave for two years, three months; defendant claimed already tried for said charges; summoned Rev. Jacob Fombon; Larken Deaver; Francis Crely.

1839

Plaintiff:	Endicott, Charles
Defendant:	Clapp, Benjamin
Plaintiff's Attorney:	Bird, Gustavus A.
Defendant's Attorney:	Risque, Ferdinand W.; Bogy, Lewis; Hunton, Logan
Verdict:	Freed
Notes:	

Plaintiff, a mulatto age eighteen, sued by next friend, Gustavus Bird; claimed kidnapped by Samuel Gray and sold to Benjamin Clapp of St. Louis; plaintiff's father, a free man of color, barbershop owner; mentioned Sackett's Harbor, New York; Brackville, Canada.

1839

Plaintiff:	Lewis
Defendant:	Stacker, John
Plaintiff's Attorney:	Risque, Ferdinand W.
Defendant's Attorney:	Darby, [John F.]

Verdict:	Not freed
Notes:	

Lewis, a minor, mother and next friend Celeste sued for freedom; grandmother Judy, aunt Aspisa, and mother all free from Judy's stay in Vincennes, Indiana, and Kaskaskia, Illinois; mentioned Pierre Menard; William Lecompte; Tousaint DuBois; Robert Bunton.

1839

Plaintiff:	Andrew
Defendant:	Sarpy, Peter
Plaintiff's Attorney:	Risque, Ferdinand W.
Defendant's Attorney:	Bogy, Lewis; Hunton, Logan
Verdict:	N/A
Notes:	

By Andrew's mother and next friend Celeste; Celeste pronounced free in St. Charles County, therefore son entitled freedom; Judy's grandson; mentioned Robert Bunton; William Sullivan; Louisville, Kentucky; Vincennes, Indiana; Kaskaskia, Illinois; Peter Menard; William LeCompte.

1839

Plaintiff:	Briscoe, Eliza
Defendant:	Anderson, William
Plaintiff's Attorney:	Risque, Ferdinand W.; Dayton, [Benjamin B.]
Defendant's Attorney:	Spalding, Josiah; Tiffany, Pardon D.
Verdict:	N/A
Notes:	

Plaintiff was moved from District of Columbia to Macomb County, Illinois, by her master Milton Walker; resided in Illinois from August 1838 to April 1839; moved to St. Louis and kept in the possession of William Anderson.

1839

Plaintiff:	Talbot, James
Defendant:	Benton, Delford; Musick, James C.; Musick, Prudence
Plaintiff's Attorney:	Bird, Gustavus A.
Defendant's Attorney:	N/A
Verdict:	N/A

Notes:

Plaintiff originally the slave of Jesse Chuck, who resided in Illinois; later taken and sold in Missouri to David Musick, now deceased; Talbot left to daughter Susan, wife of Delford Benton; plaintiff kidnapped out of jurisdiction; St. Charles Ferry; steamboat.

1839

Plaintiff:	Celeste, a woman of color
Defendant:	Papin, Alexander
Plaintiff's Attorney:	Risque, Ferdinand W.; Murdoch, Francis B.; King, [Archibald]
Defendant's Attorney:	Hudson, Thomas B.
Verdict:	N/A

Notes:

Celeste, daughter of Judy, sued for false imprisonment prior to her emancipation; Papin claimed already tried on same charges; mentioned change of venue to St. Charles County; Celeste claimed new charges and trial; included transcript of daughter Celestine's suit.

1840

Plaintiff:	Seyton
Defendant:	Littleton, William
Plaintiff's Attorney:	Bird, Gustavus A.
Defendant's Attorney:	N/A
Verdict:	Not freed

Notes:

Plaintiff also Sydney; owner George Hacker took her to southern Illinois for 3 years; gave to daughter and husband, Littleton; took her to Madison County, Illinois, for six weeks then St. Louis; includes William and Micajah Littleton's signed $500 recognizance bond.

1840

Plaintiff:	Charles
Defendant:	Verhagen, Peter; Rosati, Joseph
Plaintiff's Attorney:	Polk, Trusten; Carrol, C. C.
Defendant's Attorney:	Primm, Wilson; Taylor, [George R. or John]

Verdict: Not freed

Notes:

While plaintiff held in slavery, sent to work in Cahokia, Illinois, by owner Joseph Rosati, Bishop of St. Louis; there ten to twelve days; plaintiff held by defendant after Rosati left St. Louis; suit transferred to court of common pleas; included list of jurors.

1840

Plaintiff: Pierre

Defendant: Chouteau, Therese Cerre

Plaintiff's Attorney: Primm, Wilson

Defendant's Attorney: Spalding, Josiah; Tiffany, Pardon D.

Verdict: N/A

Notes:

Plaintiff's mother Rose born in Montreal, Canada, and lived in Prairie du Chien, Wisconsin; owners John Stork; Pierre Joseph Didier; Auguste Chouteau; Edward Chouteau, and Therese; Rose's sons, slaves Benoist and Toussaint; includes bills of sale in Spanish.

1840

Plaintiff: Barnes, Brunetta

Defendant: Meachum, John Berry

Plaintiff's Attorney: Gantt, Thomas T.; Strother, George F.

Defendant's Attorney: Spalding, Josiah; Tiffany, Pardon D.

Verdict: N/A

Notes:

Plaintiff age fourteen, by next friend Peter Charleville; sued for freedom claiming $1,000 damages; included recognizance bond by Meachum and George Trask.

1840

Plaintiff: Barnes, Archibald

Defendant: Meachum, John Berry

Plaintiff's Attorney: Gantt, Thomas T.; Strother, George F.

Defendant's Attorney: Spalding, Josiah; Tiffany, Pardon D.

Verdict: N/A

Notes:

Plaintiff age sixteen; next friend Peter Charleville; sued for freedom claiming $1,000 damages.

1840

Plaintiff:	Barnes, Archibald
Defendant:	Meachum, John Berry
Plaintiff's Attorney:	Gantt, Thomas T.
Defendant's Attorney:	N/A
Verdict:	Freed
Notes:	

Plaintiff age sixteen; next friend Peter Charleville; claimed born to free parents; mother Leah Charleville gained freedom in Brown County, Ohio; Leah and children moved to Missouri; includes warrant for plaintiff; recognizance bond by Meachum and George Trask.

1840

Plaintiff:	Barnes, Brunetta
Defendant:	Meachum, John Berry
Plaintiff's Attorney:	Gantt, Thomas T.; Strother, George F.
Defendant's Attorney:	N/A
Verdict:	Freed
Notes:	

Plaintiff age fifteen; next friend Peter Charleville; claimed born to free parents; mother Leah Charleville gained her freedom in Brown County, Ohio, while pregnant with Brunetta; Leah and children moved to Missouri; includes warrant for Brunetta from defendant.

1840

Plaintiff:	Barnes, Brunetta
Defendant:	Meachum, John Berry
Plaintiff's Attorney:	Gantt, Thomas T.
Defendant's Attorney:	N/A
Verdict:	Freed
Notes:	

Plaintiff age fifteen, next friend Peter Charleville, claimed Meachum subjected her to the "grossest insults" by requiring her to deliver milk to steamboats in the early morning hours; claimed insulted by the crew; includes warrant for possession of Brunetta.

1840

Plaintiff:	Cephas, Josiah
Defendant:	Scott, James; McConnell, Mary
Plaintiff's Attorney:	Risque, Ferdinand W.; Murdoch, Francis B.; King, Archibald
Defendant's Attorney:	Leslie, Miron; Field, [Roswell M.]
Verdict:	Not freed
Notes:	

Plaintiff two years, seven months old; suit through mother and next friend Diana; born in Maryland; owned by Ann Jane Turpin who married Delahy; moved to St. Louis; sold to Charles Collins; taken to Naples, Illinois, by Delahy; Collins claimed "fugitives"; defendant Collins's attorney.

1840

Plaintiff:	Cephas, Diana
Defendant:	Scott, James
Plaintiff's Attorney:	Risque, Ferdinand W.; Murdoch, Francis B.; King, Archibald
Defendant's Attorney:	N/A
Verdict:	Freed
Notes:	

Plaintiff, age thirty-five and of African race; claimed born in Maryland and owned by Mark Delahy who moved to Naples, Illinois; hired her out; said Murray McConnell of Jacksonville, Illinois, pretended to be owner; moved her by steamboat to St. Louis; in custody of defendant.

1841

Plaintiff:	Talbot, James
Defendant:	Benton, Delford; Musick, James C; Musick, Prudence
Plaintiff's Attorney:	Bird, Gustavus A.
Defendant's Attorney:	N/A
Verdict:	Not freed
Notes:	

Plaintiff continued suit from St. Louis Circuit Court March Term 1839 #92; claimed he was free, and imprisoned without legal cause.

1841

Plaintiff:	Thompson, Richard
Defendant:	Blount, James
Plaintiff's Attorney:	King, [Archibald]
Defendant's Attorney:	Polk, Trusten
Verdict:	Not freed
Notes:	

Plaintiff, age thirty-nine, alleged he was emancipated in will of former owner, General William Ashley of St. Louis; included petition for warrant and warrant to seize the body of plaintiff to prevent him leaving jurisdiction of the court.

1841

Plaintiff:	Alsey
Defendant:	Randolph, William
Plaintiff's Attorney:	Risque, Ferdinand W.; Murdoch, Francis B.; King, [Archibald]
Defendant's Attorney:	Spalding, Josiah; Tiffany, Pardon D.
Verdict:	Not freed
Notes:	

Plaintiff born in Kentucky; owner Zachariah Cross; given to daughter Rachel, wife of Robert Funkhouser; taken to Illinois; sold to Eli Alden in Missouri, then to defendant; mentioned Galatin, Johnson, and Edwards counties in Illinois; appealed to the Missouri Supreme Court, 1844.

1841

Plaintiff:	Scott, Louis
Defendant:	Burd, William
Plaintiff's Attorney:	Langton, Jeremiah
Defendant's Attorney:	Spalding, Josiah; Tiffany, Pardon D.
Verdict:	Not freed
Notes:	

Plaintiff Scott sent to St. Clair County, Illinois, by defendant Burd to repair "copper kettles or stills" purchased from defendant; mentioned Bernard Smelter was German, needed translator; Included bill of exceptions; appealed to Missouri Supreme Court.

1841

Plaintiff:	Charles
Defendant:	Christy, Belina
Plaintiff's Attorney:	Risque, Ferdinand W.; Murdoch, Francis B.; King, [Archibald]
Defendant's Attorney:	Spalding, Josiah; Tiffany Pardon D.
Verdict:	Not freed
Notes:	

Plaintiff age twenty-three; born in Cahokia, Illinois; mother a servant of Joseph Troke; sheriff levied on Charles on execution against Troke; sold to Alfred Cowles; Ebenezer Pickering; then Samuel Christy whose widow is defendant; venue changed to Court of Common Pleas.

1841

Plaintiff:	Brown, Squire
Defendant:	Anderson, William C.
Plaintiff's Attorney:	Dayton, Benjamin B.; Davis, [Andrew J. or Charles H.]
Defendant's Attorney:	Blair, Montgomery
Verdict:	N/A
Notes:	

Plaintiff claimed previous owner, Henry Brown, hired him out for several months at a time in St. Clair County, Illinois; worked in Illinois between 1839 and 1841; sold to defendant William B. Anderson May 1841; sued for damages of $500.

1841

Plaintiff:	Cephas, Diana
Defendant:	Scott, James
Plaintiff's Attorney:	Risque, Ferdinand W.: Murdoch, F. R.; King, Archibald
Defendant's Attorney:	Leslie, Miron
Verdict:	N/A
Notes:	

Case file contains no petition; included agreement between attorneys that Murray McConnell be substituted as defendant; that this case be combined with *Josiah Cephas v. Scott and McConnell*, November Term 1840, #361; included William Scott as a defendant.

1841

Plaintiff:	Charles
Defendant:	Verhagen, Peter
Plaintiff's Attorney:	Polk, Trusten; Carroll, C. C.
Defendant's Attorney:	Primm, Wilson
Verdict:	N/A
Notes:	

Change of venue from St. Louis Circuit Court to Court of Common Pleas; plaintiff sent to Illinois to fit a "nunnery" by former owner, Bishop Joseph Rosati; ownership transferred to Verhagen; includes copy of original Circuit Court case July Term 1840 #203.

1841

Plaintiff:	Preston; Braxton; Mary; Nat; Beverly, et al.
Defendant:	Coons, George, W., Adminstrator, et al.
Plaintiff's Attorney:	Risque, Ferdinand W.; King, [Archibald]; Townshend, [J.B.]; Goode, [George W.]; Cormick, [Tully R.]
Defendant's Attorney:	Gamble, Hamilton R.; Walker, [Joseph B.]; Darby, John F.; Knox, [Samuel]; Hudson, [Thomas B.]; Holmes, [Nathaniel]
Verdict:	N/A
Notes:	

Estate of Milton Duty; plaintiffs claimed Duty stated he had manumitted them in his will; defendants tried to sell slaves to cover Duty's alleged debt; Braxton claimed Duty stated his intention to buy property in Soulard to build cabins for his slaves; slaves Preston, Braxton, Mary, Nat, Beverly, Jesse, Jordan, Madison, Malinda, Seany, Clarissa, Caroline, Nelly, Lucy, Lydia, Harry, Henderson, Jackson, Mary, Howard, James, Lewis, Margaret, Ann Eliza, Beverly, James, Lucy Ellen.

1841

Plaintiff:	Jonathan
Defendant:	Brotherton, Marshall; Danah, Joil; Willoughby, Aza
Plaintiff's Attorney:	Murdoch, Francis B.; King, [John B. or Archibald]
Defendant's Attorney:	Geyer, Henry S.; Dayton, Benjamin B.
Verdict:	Freed
Notes:	

Plaintiff, age thirty-four, born in Virginia; owned by Edward Gleason; taken to White County, Tennessee; inherited by James Gleason; to St. Louis and Madison County, Illinois; James died; widow married Willoughby; Jonathan levied upon as Willoughby's by Brotherton after suit with Danah; Beverly, Madison, Samuel, Harry.

1842

Plaintiff:	Charles
Defendant:	Christy, Belina
Plaintiff's Attorney:	Murdoch, F.R.; Risque, Ferdinand W.; King, [Archibald]
Defendant's Attorney:	Spalding, Josiah; Tiffany, Pardon D.
Verdict:	N/A
Notes:	

Change of venue at defendant's request; plaintiff claimed born in Cahokia, Illinois; mother Joseph Troke's servant; at age eleven, levied upon by sheriff for execution against Troke; owned by Alfred Cowles; Ebenezer Pickering; Samuel Christy and widow, the defendant.

1842

Plaintiff:	Vica
Defendant:	Hobart, Samuel
Plaintiff's Attorney:	N/A
Defendant's Attorney:	N/A
Verdict:	Not freed
Notes:	

Vica, age nineteen; next friend Christy Evans; born in North Carolina; owner Isabella Walker; taken to Mississippi; willed to son Felix; worked in St. Clair and Jackson counties, Illinois, to St. Louis by Benjamin Dill, left with John Sparr, sold to Lyman B. Shaw; sold to defendant; included document tying her case to her sons, Thadeus Alonzo and Musa Ben Abel Gazen.

1842

Plaintiff:	Alonzo, Thadeus
Defendant:	Sparr, John; Hobart, Samuel; Mellody, George
Plaintiff's Attorney:	King, [John or Archibald]; Murdoch, Francis B.
Defendant's Attorney:	N/A
Verdict:	Not freed

Notes:

Plaintiff ten months old; next friend Christy Evans; mother Vica; born in Jackson County, Illinois; taken to St. Louis and left in care of Sparr; sold to Lyman B. Shaw; to Hobart; held by Mellody; claimed mother's Indian heritage; plaintiff's father white.

1842

Plaintiff:	Gazen, Musa Ben Abel
Defendant:	Sparr, John; Hobart, Samuel; Mellody, George
Plaintiff's Attorney:	Murdoch, Francis B.; King, [John or Archibald]
Defendant's Attorney:	N/A
Verdict:	Not freed
Notes:	

Plaintiff age three; next friend Christy Evans; mother Vica; taken to Jackson County, Illinois; taken to St. Louis; left in care of Sparr; sold to Lyman B. Shaw; to Hobart; held by Mellody; claimed mother's Indian heritage; plaintiff's father white.

1842

Plaintiff:	Jackson, Jinny
Defendant:	Fraser, James O.
Plaintiff's Attorney:	Walker, Joseph B.; Gamble, Hamilton R.
Defendant's Attorney:	Polk, Trusten
Verdict:	Freed
Notes:	

Plaintiff age fifty-five; claimed entitled freedom at age twenty-one from mother, Pegg's, manumission deed; original owner Richard Dallam; includes manumission deed dated 1787; slaves Judith, Poll, Dick, Andrew, Sall, Grace, Fanney listed with Pegg.

1842

Plaintiff:	Jackson, Henry
Defendant:	Fraser, James O.
Plaintiff's Attorney:	Walker, Joseph B.; Gamble, Hamilton R.
Defendant's Attorney:	Polk, Trusten
Verdict:	Freed
Notes:	

Includes petition of Henry, Margaret, and Sally Jackson children of Jinny; Anna Maria, William Henry, and Smith children of Margaret; entitled freedom from deed of manumission for Jinny and grandmother Pegg; dated 1787 by Richard Dallam.

1842

Plaintiff:	Ann Maria
Defendant:	Fraser, James O.
Plaintiff's Attorney:	Walker, Joseph B.; Gamble, Hamilton R.
Defendant's Attorney:	Polk, Trusten
Verdict:	Freed
Notes:	

Declaration of plaintiff of trespass, assault, and false imprisonment by defendant; sought damages of $500.

1842

Plaintiff:	Jackson, Sally
Defendant:	Fraser, James O.
Plaintiff's Attorney:	Walker, Joseph B.; Gamble, Hamilton R.
Defendant's Attorney:	Polk, Trusten
Verdict:	Freed
Notes:	

Declaration of plaintiff of trespass, assault, and false imprisonment by defendant; sought damages of $500.

1842

Plaintiff:	Jackson, Margaret
Defendant:	Fraser, James O.
Plaintiff's Attorney:	Walker, Joseph B.; Gamble, Hamilton R.
Defendant's Attorney:	Polk, Trusten
Verdict:	Freed
Notes:	

Declaration of plaintiff of trespass, assault, and false imprisonment by defendant; sought damages of $500.

1842

Plaintiff:	William, Henry
Defendant:	Fraser, James O.
Plaintiff's Attorney:	Walker, Joseph B.; Gamble, Hamilton R.
Defendant's Attorney:	Polk, Trusten
Verdict:	Freed
Notes:	

Declaration of plaintiff of trespass, assault, and false imprisonment by defendant; sought damages of $500.

1842

Plaintiff:	Smith
Defendant:	Fraser, James O.
Plaintiff's Attorney:	Walker, Joseph B.; Gamble, Hamilton R.
Defendant's Attorney:	Polk, Trusten
Verdict:	Freed
Notes:	

Declaration of plaintiff of trespass, assault, and false imprisonment by defendant; sought damages of $500.

1842

Plaintiff:	Pierre
Defendant:	Chouteau, Gabriel
Plaintiff's Attorney:	Primm, Wilson; Murdoch, Francis B.; Taylor, George R.; Hall; Field, [George B.]
Defendant's Attorney:	Spalding, Josiah; Tiffany, Pardon D.
Verdict:	Not freed
Notes:	

Plaintiff's mother Rose born in Montreal, Canada and lived in Prairie du Chien, Wisconsin; owners John Stork; Pierre Joseph Didier; Auguste Chouteau; Auguste's widow Therese and defendant; Rose's sons Benoist and Toussaint; mentioned Indian slavery "panis"; slaves Hanover, Jack, Louisa, Joseph, Jacques, Charlotte, Caesar; includes copy of Habeas Corpus case Robin, alias Robert; 1763 British Treaty; Acts of George III 1790 and 1793; deposition in French; bill of sale; agreement to use depositions in November Term 1843 case #13, April Term 1844 cases #51 and #151.

1843

Plaintiff:	Jefferson, Thomas
Defendant:	Hopkins, Milton W.
Plaintiff's Attorney:	Murdoch, Francis B.; Dawson, Andrew H. H.; Field, Roswell, M.
Defendant's Attorney:	Leslie, Miron; Lord
Verdict:	N/A
Notes:	

Plaintiff age thirty-two; born a slave in Virginia; brought by owner Charles Drexler to St. Louis; sold to Samuel Prosser; taken to Morgan County, Illinois; sold to defendants after previous suit had commenced.

1843

Plaintiff:	Rebecca
Defendant:	Black, James; Horine, Thomas; Melody, George
Plaintiff's Attorney:	Risk, Thomas F.; Murdoch, Francis B.
Defendant's Attorney:	Allen, Beverly
Verdict:	Not freed
Notes:	

Plaintiff age twenty-two; previous case ruled nonsuit per negligence of attorney Harris L. Sproat; owned by Judge William James of Ste. Genevieve; Black moved her to Vandalia, Illinois; hired out in Kaskaskia, Illinois; arrested by Horine, Black's brother-in-law; jailor Mellody.

1843

Plaintiff:	Brown, Squire
Defendant:	Anderson, C.R.; Morris, S.
Plaintiff's Attorney:	Dayton, Benjamin. B.
Defendant's Attorney:	Todd, Albert; Krumm, John M.
Verdict:	N/A
Notes:	

Plaintiff claimed a previous owner, Henry Brown, hired him out in St. Clair County, Illinois, for months at a time; claimed Anderson attempted to remove him downriver to New Orleans, out of the jurisdiction of the court; Morris also identified as owner.

1843

Plaintiff:	Catharine, Felix; William; Minta
Defendant:	Hundley, Thomas; Pattison, D.; Russell, William
Plaintiff's Attorney:	Blennerhassett, Richard S.
Defendant's Attorney:	Drake, Charles D.; Rannells, Charles S.
Verdict:	Not freed
Notes:	

Plaintiffs claimed given deed of emancipation by previous owner Eli West in 1840; Felix son of Catharine; claimed defendants arrested them illegally; further stated claim for freedom by noting their residence in Ohio.

1843

Plaintiff:	Celeste, a woman of color
Defendant:	Papin, Alexander
Plaintiff's Attorney:	Risque, Ferdinand W.; Murdoch, Francis B.; King, [Archibald]
Defendant's Attorney:	Hudson, Thomas B.
Verdict:	N/A
Notes:	

Celeste, daughter of Judy, sued for false imprisonment prior to her emancipation; Papin claimed already tried on same charges; mentioned change of venue to St. Charles County; Celeste claimed new charges and trial; included transcript of daughter Celestine's suit.

1844

Plaintiff:	Chouteau, Louis
Defendant:	Chouteau, Gabriel
Plaintiff's Attorney:	Duncan, J. McKim; Cobb, Henry L.; Shreve, Luther M.; Boyer
Defendant's Attorney:	Spalding, Josiah; Tiffany, Pardon D.
Verdict:	Freed
Notes:	

Plaintiff son of Rose; suit based on Rose's Canadian birth and Prairie du Chien, Wisconsin residence; mentioned John Storke; Andrew Todd; Joseph Didier; Auguste Chouteau; defendant purchased plaintiff at Chouteau's estate sale; case litigated through Civil War; included record of account of costs; statement of Bernard M. Lynch concerning plaintiff; depositions used from November Term 1842 #125.

1844

Plaintiff:	Paschall, Andrian
Defendant:	Ulrici, Richard W.
Plaintiff's Attorney:	Carr, Levi T.
Defendant's Attorney:	Spalding, Josiah; Tiffany, Pardon D.
Verdict:	N/A
Notes:	

Plaintiff claimed former owner Gabriel Paul sent him to Illinois; included deposition from Paul stating he purchased plaintiff from estate sale of Auguste Chouteau; Paul sent Michel to Rocky Mountains on hire; included bill of sale from Paul to Ulrici.

1844

Plaintiff:	Nat
Defendant:	Coons, George W.
Plaintiff's Attorney:	Risque, Ferdinand W.; Townsend, James B.
Defendant's Attorney:	Walker, Joseph B.; Hudson, Thomas B.
Verdict:	Not freed
Notes:	

Plaintiff claimed former owner, Milton Duty, now deceased, manumitted him and others in his will dated 1836; 1837 Duty moved his slaves to Missouri; died 1838; will from probate of Warren County, Missouri; includes bill of exceptions with description of testimony of Richard Dowling, David Adams, and J.V. Prather; three copies of Duty's Will, endorsed by St. Louis probate; copy of Duty's inventory of property; copy of account; mentioned slaves Maria, Ann, Milly and her five children; Charity, Nat, Olivia, Braxton, Preston, Louisa, Malinda, Howard, Sena (also Seany); Clarissa, Ann Eliza, Lucy, Mary, Louisa, Mary, Beverly, Alfred, Sam, Carolin, Ellen, Jesse, Lydia, Nelly, Elizabeth, Jordan, Madison, Henderson, Harry, Charlotty, Harrison, and Amanda.

1844

Plaintiff:	Britton, Lucy Ann (Delaney)
Defendant:	Mitchell, David D.
Plaintiff's Attorney:	Murdoch, Francis B.
Defendant's Attorney:	Spalding, Josiah; Tiffany, Pardon D.
Verdict:	N/A
Notes:	

Plaintiff by her mother and next friend Polly Wash sued for freedom; declaration of trespass; damages of $1,000; no petition included.

1844

Plaintiff:	Celestine
Defendant:	Dumont, Julia
Plaintiff's Attorney:	Murdoch, Francis B.
Defendant's Attorney:	Primm, Wilson; Taylor, George R.
Verdict:	Not freed
Notes:	

Plaintiff age thirty-six; claimed mother Sally born in Kaskaskia, Illinois, after the Ordinance of 1787; plaintiff taken by former owner, Madam Deroine, to Cahokia, Illinois; sold to Julia Buson, who married Charles Dumont.

1844

Plaintiff:	Preston
Defendant:	Coons, George W.
Plaintiff's Attorney:	Risque, Ferdinand W.; Townsend, James B.
Defendant's Attorney:	Walker, Joseph B.; Hudson, Thomas B.
Verdict:	N/A
Notes:	

Plaintiff claimed former owner, Milton Duty, now deceased, manumitted him and others in his will dated 1836; 1837 Duty moved his slaves to Missouri; died 1838; will from probate of Warren County, Mississippi.

1844

Plaintiff:	Smith, Cloe Ann
Defendant:	Knox, Franklin
Plaintiff's Attorney:	Field, [Roswell M.]; Murdoch, Francis B.
Defendant's Attorney:	Knox, Thomas M.
Verdict:	Not freed
Notes:	

Plaintiff taken to Huron County, Ohio, by Knox's wife, with his consent; mentioned Ordinance of 1787; alleged she was about to be sold out of jurisdiction.

1844

Plaintiff:	Moore, Amy
Defendant:	Moore, Robert N.
Plaintiff's Attorney:	Smith, Elias B.
Defendant's Attorney:	Risk, Thomas F.; Morehead, Philip C.
Verdict:	Not freed

Notes:

Plaintiff claimed hired out to Mr. Marbly for two years in Springfield, Illinois, by former master; afterward sold to defendant in St. Louis; defendant noted obtained Amy after her owner Cartright had been detained in Illinois over shooting a man.

1844

Plaintiff:	Hannah
Defendant:	Pitcher, John
Plaintiff's Attorney:	Murdoch, Francis B.
Defendant's Attorney:	N/A
Verdict:	Freed

Notes:

Plaintiff brought suit again after case dismissed ten days earlier; requested a warrant for herself, due to maltreatment as a result of her previous suit; former owner Daniel Page and wife took her to Boston, Massachusetts; defendant bought her upon return to St. Louis; included bill of exceptions with description of testimony of Mrs. Page, Samuel Knox, and J. R. Shepley.

1844

Plaintiff:	James
Defendant:	Cordell, Hiram
Plaintiff's Attorney:	Field, Roswell M.
Defendant's Attorney:	Tarver, Micajah
Verdict:	Freed

Notes:

Plaintiff age nine; son of Martha Ann, whose petition referenced in his petition; claimed born free, as his mother was entitled her freedom; owned by Sarah Young; defendant was administrator of Young's estate.

1844

Plaintiff:	Hannah
Defendant:	Pitcher, John
Plaintiff's Attorney:	Murdoch, Francis B.
Defendant's Attorney:	Primm, Wilson; Taylor, George R.
Verdict:	N/A
Notes:	

Plaintiff age nineteen; sued by next friend Charles Edmon; former owner Daniel D. Page and his wife took her to Boston, Massachusetts; plaintiff remembered same year a Catholic convent burned by mob in Charleston; sold to defendant upon return to St. Louis.

1844

Plaintiff:	Martha Ann
Defendant:	Cordell, Hiram
Plaintiff's Attorney:	Field, Roswell M.
Defendant's Attorney:	Tarver, Micajah; [Hempstead, Charles S.]
Verdict:	Freed
Notes:	

Plaintiff born in St. Louis; owned by Dr. John Young; taken to Galena, Illinois, to work as domestic; moved to Alabama, where Young died; widow Sarah moved to St. Louis, where she died; defendant administrator of Sarah's estate; included list of jurors.

1844

Plaintiff:	Drusella, Martha
Defendant:	Curle, Richmond, L.
Plaintiff's Attorney:	Murdoch, Francis B.; Primm, Wilson; Taylor, George R.
Defendant's Attorney:	Hudson, Thomas B.
Verdict:	Freed
Notes:	

Plaintiff claimed born free in Lawrence County, Alabama; argued she had "not one fourth Negro blood in her veins"; indentured to John Cotton at age one by mother Malinda; taken to Arkansas; upon Cotton's death, the Isbels, his son-in-law's family, attempted to sell plaintiff in Missouri; placed her with Felix Coontz who placed her with defendant; included $500 recognizance bond.

1844

Plaintiff:	Speaks, Mary Ann
Defendant:	Quissenbury, James; Jameson, John
Plaintiff's Attorney:	Primm, Wilson; Taylor, George R.
Defendant's Attorney:	Lackland, Benjamin E.
Verdict:	N/A
Notes:	

Plaintiff age twenty-four; claimed born free; indentured to Susan Blunt of Alexandria County, District of Columbia; alleged Blunt agreed to subtract two years from indenture if Mary came to St. Louis; Blunt died; Quissenburry administrator to estate; Jameson was jailor; included affadavit stating the terms of indenture dated 1838; named Mary's mother as Mary Turly, a slave.

1845

Plaintiff:	Robinson, Mary
Defendant:	Watson, Ringrose D.; Corson, Amos
Plaintiff's Attorney:	Smith, [Elias B. or Sol]; Langton, Jeremiah
Defendant's Attorney:	Crockett, J. B.; Briggs, [David C. or T. C.]
Verdict:	Not freed
Notes:	

Plaintiff's name also spelled Robertson; taken to Alton, Illinois, by owner Corson; sent to St. Louis where held by Watson; previous suit filed 1841 dismissed because Watson denied ownership of plaintiff; claimed damages of $500.

1845

Plaintiff:	Paul, Mitchell
Defendant:	Paul, Adolph, Administrator
Plaintiff's Attorney:	Duncan, J. McKim; Cobb, Henry L.
Defendant's Attorney:	Spalding, Josiah; Tiffany, Pardon D.
Verdict:	N/A
Notes:	

Estate of Gabriel Paul; plaintiff initiated suit for freedom in April Term 1844 against Gabriel Paul; since then, Paul died; mentioned Pierre and Louis, waiting for the Supreme Court's decisions in those cases for final decision in Michel's.

1845

Plaintiff:	Hicks, Elsa
Defendant:	Burrell, S; Mitchell, Louis
Plaintiff's Attorney:	King, John B.; Risk, Thomas F.
Defendant's Attorney:	N/A
Verdict:	N/A
Notes:	

Plaintiff age twenty-one; born in Virginia; acquired by James Mitchell through marriage; claimed taken by Mitchell to Wisconsin Territory to work; taken to St. Louis where hired out to Edward Gay; held by Mitchell's brother-in-law, S. Burrell; Ordinance of 1787.

1845

Plaintiff:	Steele, Rachel
Defendant:	Taylor, Thomas
Plaintiff's Attorney:	Field, Roswell M.
Defendant's Attorney:	N/A
Verdict:	Not freed
Notes:	

Plaintiff owned by late Samuel Gilbert; hired out in Keokuk, Iowa, to Russell Farnham; upon Gilbert's death, claimed by husband of Gilbert's granddaughter, Thomas Taylor; included letter of reference from Charlotte P. Grimes claiming the plaintiff to be an "honest and upright woman"; instructed further recommendation to be addressed to her husband, William L. Grimes, of steamboat *Uncle Toby*.

1846

Plaintiff:	Scott, Dred
Defendant:	Emerson, Irene
Plaintiff's Attorney:	N/A
Defendant's Attorney:	N/A
Verdict:	Not freed
Notes:	

These documents are part of the Dred Scott case; plaintiff married to Harriet Scott; court dealt with cases in tandem; second suit filed in November Term 1847 #19, but plaintiffs agreed to withdraw these and continue with the unresolved first case.

1846

Plaintiff:	Scott, Harriet
Defendant:	Emerson, Irene
Plaintiff's Attorney:	N/A
Defendant's Attorney:	N/A
Verdict:	Not freed
Notes:	

These documents are part of the Dred Scott case; plaintiff married to Dred Scott; court dealt with cases in tandem; second suit filed in November Term 1847 #20, but plaintiffs agreed to withdraw these and continue with the unresolved first case.

1846

Plaintiff:	Thomas, Matilda
Defendant:	Littleton, William
Plaintiff's Attorney:	Hall, D. W.
Defendant's Attorney:	Primm, Wilson; Taylor, Pardon D.
Verdict:	N/A
Notes:	

Plaintiff also known as Matilda Cunningham; included plea; claimed defendant had imprisoned her for one year and again for 6 months; motion from defendant asking suit to be dismissed on grounds plaintiff had not put up a security for the case's costs.

1846

Plaintiff:	Littleton, Missouri
Defendant:	Littleton, William
Plaintiff's Attorney:	Hall, D W
Defendant's Attorney:	Primm, Wilson; Taylor, Pardon D.
Verdict:	N/A
Notes:	

Plaintiff declared plea of trespass and false imprisonment; claimed defendant had imprisoned her for one year and again for six months; motion from defendant asking suit to be dismissed on grounds plaintiff had not put up a security for the case's costs.

1846

Plaintiff:	Gabriel
Defendant:	Christy, Andrew, Executor; Coons, Mary, Executrix
Plaintiff's Attorney:	Shepley, John R.
Defendant's Attorney:	Spalding, Josiah; Tiffany, Pardon D.
Verdict:	N/A
Notes:	

Plaintiff entered plea of trespass; estate of David Coons; includes copy of note from probate stating Gabriel had entered an agreement with David Coons, deceased, to purchase his freedom; mentioned bill of sale in which Coons, Gabriel, and former master McClelland acknowledged Gabriel putting up some of the money for the sale and commitment to pay the remainder.

1848

Plaintiff:	Nancy
Defendant:	Steen, Enoch
Plaintiff's Attorney:	Dick, F. A.; Farrar, Benjamin
Defendant's Attorney:	Gantt, Thomas T.
Verdict:	Freed
Notes:	

Plaintiff born in Territory of Florida; claimed grandmother was an Indian and mother free; taken by Capt. John Page, 4th Infantry, at age ten to live with him as free; Aenus McKay took her after Page died; defendant then took her and held her as a slave; depositions placed plaintiff in Alabama living with the Creek Nation at Fort Mitchell; claimed heard speaking "Indian tongue" and wearing Indian dress; lived at Jefferson Barracks during trial.

1848

Plaintiff:	Scott, Thomas
Defendant:	Harrison, James
Plaintiff's Attorney:	Wright, [Uriel]; Bowman, Samuel M.
Defendant's Attorney:	Geyer, Henry S.; Dayton, Benjamin B.
Verdict:	Not freed
Notes:	

Plaintiff claimed defendant hired him out to Ceran St. Vrain; St. Vrain, employed as a trader, took plaintiff to the "country of New Mexico" in 1847; deposition by

St. Vrain claimed plaintiff was hired out because Harrison desired plaintiff's health to improve.

1848

Plaintiff:	Perryman, Peggy
Defendant:	Philibert, Joseph
Plaintiff's Attorney:	Shreve, Luther M.
Defendant's Attorney:	Field, [George B. or Alexander P.]; Hall
Verdict:	Not freed
Notes:	

Plaintiff claimed born free in Arkansas; father was a "free person of color," mother an Indian of the Blackfoot tribe, "legally married"; claimed siezed, bound and gagged, sold into slavery in Missouri; mother's family has been "free since the memory of man"; includes bill of exception.

1850

Plaintiff:	Duty, Harry
Defendant:	Darby, John F., Administrator
Plaintiff's Attorney:	Field, Alexander P.; Hall
Defendant's Attorney:	Harney, Thomas
Verdict:	Not freed
Notes:	

Plaintiff a slave of Milton Duty, deceased 1838; claimed Duty freed him and others in his will; defendant administrator to Duty's estate.

1850

Plaintiff:	Duty, Nelly
Defendant:	Darby, John F., Administrator
Plaintiff's Attorney:	Field, Alexander P.; Hall
Defendant's Attorney:	Harney, Thomas
Verdict:	Not freed
Notes:	

Plaintiff a slave of Milton Duty, deceased 1838; claimed Duty freed her and others in his will; defendant administrator to Duty's estate; motion by defendant to dismiss case for lack of security by plaintiff.

1850

Plaintiff:	Duty, Preston
Defendant:	Darby, John F., Administrator
Plaintiff's Attorney:	Field, Alexander P.; Hall
Defendant's Attorney:	Harney, Thomas
Verdict:	Not freed
Notes:	

Plaintiff a slave of Milton Duty, deceased 1838; claimed Duty freed him and others in his will; defendant adminstrator to Duty's estate; motion by defendant to dismiss case for lack of security by plaintiff.

1850

Plaintiff:	Duty, Lucinda
Defendant:	Darby, John F., Administrator
Plaintiff's Attorney:	Field, Alexander P.; Hall
Defendant's Attorney:	Harney, Thomas
Verdict:	Not freed
Notes:	

Plaintiff a slave of Milton Duty, deceased 1838; claimed Duty freed her and others in his will; defendant adminstrator to Duty's estate; motion by defendant to dismiss case for lack of security by plaintiff.

1850

Plaintiff:	Duty, Mary
Defendant:	Darby, John F., Administrator
Plaintiff's Attorney:	Field, Alexander P.; Hall
Defendant's Attorney:	Harney, Thomas
Verdict:	Not freed
Notes:	

Plaintiff a slave of Milton Duty, deceased 1838; claimed Duty freed her and others in his will; defendant adminstrator to Duty's estate; motion by defendant to dismiss case for lack of security by plaintiff.

1850

Plaintiff:	Duty, Caroline
Defendant:	Darby, John F., Administrator
Plaintiff's Attorney:	Field, Alexander P.; Hall
Defendant's Attorney:	Harney, Thomas
Verdict:	Not freed
Notes:	

Plaintiff a slave of Milton Duty, deceased 1838; claimed Duty freed her and others in his will; defendant adminstrator to Duty's estate; motion by defendant to dismiss case for lack of security by plaintiff.

1850

Plaintiff:	Duty, Ellen
Defendant:	Darby, John F., Administrator
Plaintiff's Attorney:	Field, Alexander P.; Hall
Defendant's Attorney:	Harney, Thomas
Verdict:	Not freed
Notes:	

Plaintiff a slave of Milton Duty, deceased 1838; claimed Duty freed her and others in his will; defendant adminstrator to Duty's estate; motion by defendant to dismiss case for lack of security by plaintiff.

1850

Plaintiff:	Duty, Jordan
Defendant:	Darby, John F., Administrator
Plaintiff's Attorney:	Field, Alexander P.; Hall
Defendant's Attorney:	Harney, Thomas
Verdict:	Not freed
Notes:	

Plaintiff a slave of Milton Duty, deceased 1838; claimed Duty freed him and others in his will; defendant adminstrator to Duty's estate; motion by defendant to dismiss case for lack of security by plaintiff; note permitting dismissal of suits by Jordan, Caroline, Preston, Mary, Nelly, Ellen, Harry, and "one other not remembered."

1852

Plaintiff:	Gabriel
Defendant:	Wiles, Michael
Plaintiff's Attorney:	Goff, James B.
Defendant's Attorney:	Todd, Albert; Krumm, John M.
Verdict:	Not freed
Notes:	

Plaintiff claimed defendant took him to Territory of California in 1850; claimed held him there as a resident for three months or more.

1853

Plaintiff:	Kinney, Thornton
Defendant:	Hatcher, John F.; Bridges, Charles C.
Plaintiff's Attorney:	Williams; Bay [W.V.N.]
Defendant's Attorney:	N/A
Verdict:	N/A
Notes:	

Plaintiff arrested as runaway; claimed by John F. Hatcher of New Orleans; plaintiff claimed born free in Albemarle County, Virginia; mother of Indian descent; apprentice to J. J. Kennedy, a tanner and shoemaker in Stanton, Virginia; at age twenty-one given free papers by guardian Samuel Clark; left Virginia to work on steamboats in the West and South; became acquainted with Rev. Robert Finley, an agent of the American Colonization Society; convinced plaintiff to go to Liberia on ship *Monrovia*; lived there five years; threw away freedom papers in Liberia; came back to United States; served on ships *Cipher* and *Leonidas*; registered a letter from the colonial secretary of Sierra Leone in lieu of freedom papers at Louisville, Kentucky, and New Orleans, Louisiana; worked on steamboats *Die Vernon, St. Louis, Buena Vista, Caddo*; captain of *Caddo* attempted to enslave plaintiff, but escaped; married a free woman and settled in St. Louis; brother John Kinney a cooper in Cincinnati; letter from plaintiff's lawyers requesting clothing for plaintiff; included bill of sale from crew of *Caddo* to defendant Bridges.

1859

Plaintiff:	Clinton, Richard
Defendant:	Blackburn, John Edward, Martha A., Charles A., and Rufus C.; Edward Hall, Curator
Plaintiff's Attorney:	Woodson, Richard G.; Bates, [Edward R.]
Defendant's Attorney:	N/A
Verdict:	N/A

Notes:

Estates of Martha A., Charles A., and Rufus C. Blackburn; plaintiff also known as Clinton; claimed he was manumitted by his previous owner Lewis James's will; Lewis died 1830, but set condition that Richard would be free after the death of Lewis's parents, Morris and Catherine James, or upon attaining twenty-one years of age; Morris and Catherine died 1834 and 1838; Clinton age twenty-one in 1844 or 1845, yet still a slave; note from defendant Edward Hall claiming he was no longer curator of said estates.

ENDNOTES

1. The Eighth Congress of the United States passed legislation titled "An Act Erecting Louisiana into two territories, and providing for the temporary government thereof," on March 26, 1804.
2. William Hyde, ed., *Encyclopedia of the History of St. Louis* (New York: Southern History Co., 1899), 2241; Harriet C. Frazier, *Slavery and Crime in Missouri, 1773-1865* (Jefferson, N.C.: McFarland and Company, Inc. 2001), 27-28.
3. J. Thomas Scharf, *History of Saint Louis City and County, From the Earliest Periods to the Present Day: Including Biographical Sketches of Representative Men*, Volume II (Philadelphia: Louis H. Everts & Co., 1883).
4. Perry McCandless and William E. Foley, *Missouri: Then and Now* (Columbia: University of Missouri, 1992), 68.
5. Scott K. Williams, "Slavery in St. Louis" (2006), www.usgennet.org/usa/mo/county/stlouis/slavery.htm.
6. Stuart Banner, *Legal Systems in Conflict, Property and Sovereignty in Missouri, 1750-1850* (Norman: University of Oklahoma Press, 2000), 106.
7. Banner, *Legal Systems in Conflict*, 104-105; Stuart Banner, *Why Lawyers Came to Missouri, Legal Systems in Conflict* (Norman: University of Oklahoma Press, 2000), 105.
8. *New York Times*, March 7, 1874.
9. Edlie L. Wong, *Neither Slave Nor Free* (New York: New York University Press, 2009), 150.
10. *Quarterly Journal of the Missouri Historical Society*, St. Louis, Vol. 14-15, 8.
11. Private papers of Albert Jefferson, "The Negro of Carondelet" (Courtesy of the Carondelet Historical Society), 55.
12. John Aaron Wright, *St. Louis: Disappearing Black Communities* (Mount Pleasant, S.C.: Arcadia Press, 2005).
13. Hyde, *Encyclopedia of the History of St. Louis*.
14. William Van Ness Bay, *Reminiscences of the Bench and Bar of Missouri* (St. Louis: F. H. Thomas and Company, 1878), 277-280.
15. Charles Van Ravenswaay, *St. Louis: An Informal History of the City and Its People, 1764-1865* (St. Louis, Missouri Historical Society Press, 1991), 202.
16. Hyde, *Encyclopedia of the History of St. Louis*, 1234.
17. Scharf, *History of Saint Louis City and County*, 1461.
18. *Missouri Republican*, July 9, 1823.
19. St. Louis County Probate Court files, Estate #587-B.
20. Allan Nevins, *The War for the Union: War Becomes Revolution, 1862-1863* (New York: Scribner, 1960), 313.
21. *New York Times*, February 17, 1860.
22. William S. Bryan and Robert Rose, *A History of the Pioneer Families of Missouri* (Santa Monica, Calif.: Janaway Publishing, 2011).
23. Doris Kearns Goodwin, *A Team of Rivals* (New York: Simon & Schuster, 2005), 63.
24. Letter from Barton Bates to Edward Bates, May 13, 1864, Missouri Historical Museum archives.
25. Opinion of Attorney General Edward Bates on citizenship, Government Printing Office, 1862.

26. David M. Silver, *Lincoln's Supreme Court* (Champaign: University of Illinois Press, 1998), 196; Helen Nicolay, "Lincoln's Cabinet," *The Abraham Lincoln Quarterly* (March 1949), 290.
27. Doug Linder, "The Trial of the Lincoln Assassination Conspirators," 2009, law2.umkc. edu/faculty/projects/ftrials/lincolnconspiracy/lincolnaccount.html.
28. *New York Times*, May 28, 1869.
29. St. Louis Circuit Court Probate Court Estate #2331, opened February 27, 1847.
30. Charlotte Taylor Blow Charless, *A Biographical Sketch of the Life and Character of Joseph Charless* (St. Louis: A. F. Cox, Printer, Office of the Missouri Presbyterian, 1869), 2-3.
31. *Missouri Gazette*, July 6, 1808.
32. *New York Times*, June 8, 1859.
33. *New York Times*, June 8, 1859.
34. *New York Times*, November 16, 1859.
35. Scharf, *History of Saint Louis City and County*, 1455-1456.
36. Bruce Campbell Adamson, William Foley, Pam Kenny, *For Which We Stand: The Life and Papers of Rufus Easton* (Bruce Campbell Adamson Books, 1996).
37. Bay, *Reminiscences of the Bench and Bar of Missouri*, 87.
38. Adamson, *For Which We Stand*.
39. Adamson, *For Which We Stand*.
40. Hyde, *The Encyclopedia of the History of St. Louis*.
41. Scharf, *History of Saint Louis City and County*, 1483.
42. Scharf, *History of Saint Louis City and County*, 1483.
43. Peter Shinkle, "19th Century Lawyer Is Big Gun in Concealed Carry Battle," *St. Louis Post-Dispatch*, October 25, 2003.
44. Scharf, *History of Saint Louis City and County*, 1461-1463.
45. *St. Louis Globe*, March 7, 1859.
46. St. Louis Circuit Court Probate Court, Estate #5477, opened October 24, 1859.
47. David Koenig, "Long Road to Dred Scott," *UMKC Law Review* 75, no. 1 (fall 2006).
48. Hyde, *The Encyclopedia of the History of St. Louis*.
49. Scharf, *History of Saint Louis City and County*, 1483.
50. *Rachel v. Walker*, 4 Mo. R. 350 (1835).
51. William V.N. Bay, *Reminiscences of the Bench and Bar of Missouri* (St. Louis: F.H. Thomas and Company 1878), 98-100.
52. Bay, *Reminiscences of the Bench and Bar of Missouri*, 324-330.
53. The information as to the details of the individual suits is based on the original documents maintained by the Missouri Secretary of State Archives in St. Louis.
54. Slave inventory in probate estate of Bishop Joseph Rosati, St. Louis Circuit Court Probate Estate #1887, filed May 4, 1844.
55. Mark L. Shurtleff, *Am I Not A Man? The Dred Scott Story* (Gilbert, Ariz.: Sortis Publishing, 2010); Harry Levins, "One Man's Case and How It Changed a Nation," *St. Louis Post-Dispatch*, March 3, 2007: Robert Moore Jr., "A Ray of Hope, Extinguished," *Gateway Heritage* (Winter, 1993-94); Corinne J. Naden and Rose Blue, *Dred Scott: Person Or Property?* (Oregon City, Oreg.: Marshall Cavendish, 2004); Chief Justice Michael A. Wolff, "Race, Law and the Struggle for Equality, Chief Justice Looks at Missouri Law, Politics and the Dred Scott Case," a transcript of comments made by the Chief Justice on March 1, 2007, at Washington University; *Frank Leslie's Illustrated Newspaper*, Saturday, June 27, 1857; and the original Missouri and Supreme Court decisions at *Scott v. Emerson*, 15 Mo. 576, 1853 WL 4171 (1852); *Dred Scott, Plaintiff in Error v. John Sandford*, 60 U.S. 393, 19 How. 393, 15 L.Ed. 691 (1856).
56. The majority of the information comes from the original source documents, maintained by the Missouri Secretary of State Archives in St. Louis.

57. *Winney v. Whitesides*, 1 Mo. 472 (1824).

58. Private papers of Albert Jefferson, "The Negro of Carondelet" (Courtesy of the Carondelet Historical Society). See also oral history t-0029 interview with Albert Jefferson interviewed by Dr. Richard Resh and Franklin Rother black community leaders project, August 10, 1970.

59. *Scott v. Emerson*, 15 Mo. 576, 1853 WL 4171, page 6 (1852).

60. *Rachel v. Walker*, 4 Mo. R. 350 (1836).

61. Ibid.

62. Lea VanderVelde, *Mrs. Dred Scott, A Life on Slavery's Frontier* (New York: Oxford University Press, 2009), 251; 11 Mo. 193 (1847).

63. *Rachel v. Stockton*, 9 Mo. 3 (1845).

64. To see the daughter's narrative, read Lucy A. Delaney, *From the Darkness Cometh the Light, or Struggles for Freedom* (St. Louis: J.T. Smith, 1891).

65. *Marie Charlotte v. Chouteau*, 21 Mo. 590 (1855).

66. *Mary Charlotte v. Chouteau*, 25 Mo. 465 (1857).

67. *LaGrange v. Chouteau*, 2 Mo. Rep 19 (1828).

BIBLIOGRAPHY

"A General and Public Nature of District of Louisiana of the Territory of Louisiana of the Territory of Missouri and of the State of Missouri up to the year 1824." Published under the Authority of the State of Missouri by virtue of the act to provide for the publication of certain laws approved February 13, 1839, Printed by W. Lusk and Son, 1842.

Adamson, Bruce Campbell, William Foley, Pam Kenny. *For Which We Stand: The Life and Papers of Rufus Easton* (Bruce Campbell Adamson Books, 1996).

Ayers, Edward L. *In the Presence of Mine Enemies: The Civil War in the Heart of America, 1859-1863* (New York: Norton, 2003).

Banner, Stuart. *Legal Systems in Conflict, Property and Sovereigny in Missouri, 1750 - 1850* (Norman: University of Oklahoma Press, 2000).

Beale, Howard K., ed. *Diary of Edward Bates, 1859-1866* (Washington, D.C.: United States Printing Office, 1933).

Billon, F. L. *Annals of St. Louis in Its Territorial Days* (St. Louis: F.L. Billon, 1888).

Boman, Dennis K. *Lincoln's Resolute Unionist: Hamilton Gamble, Dred Scott Dissenter and Missouri's Civil War Governor* (Baton Rouge: Louisiana University Press, 2006).

Cain, Marvin R. *Lincoln's Attorney General, Edward Bates of Missouri* (Columbia: University of Missouri Press, 1965).

Chouteau v. Marguerite, 37 U. S. 507 (1838).

Claycomb, William B. *President Lincoln and the Magoffin Brothers* (Seattle: Morningside Press, 2009).

Daily Missouri Democrat, March 8, 1859.

Foley, William E. "Slave Freedom Suits Before Dred Scott: The Case of Marie Jean Scypion's Descendants," *Missouri Historical Review,* vol. 79, no. 1, October 1984.

Frazier, Harriet C. *Slavery and Crime in Missouri, 1773-1865* (Jefferson, N.C.: McFarland and Company, Inc. 2001).

Hodes, Frederick A. *Beyond the Frontier: A History of St. Louis to 1821* (Tooele, Utah: The Patrice Press, 2004).

Hodes, Frederick A. *Rising on the River: St. Louis 1822 to 1850: Explosive Growth from town to City* (Tooele, Utah: The Patrice Press, 2009).

Hyde, William & Howard L. Conrad *Encyclopedia of the History of St. Louis* (New York: Southern History Co., 1899).

Journal and proceedings of the Missouri State Convention: Held at Jefferson City and St. Louis, March, 1861 (G. Knapp, 1861).

Kearns Goodwin, Doris. *Team of Rivals* (New York: Simon Schuster, 2005).

Koenig, David. *Long Road to Dred Scott.*

Missouri Republican, July 2, 1823.

Missouri Republican, July 9, 1823.

Missouri Republican, July 23, 1823.

Missouri Republican, July 20, 1826.

Missouri Republican, September 28, 1826.

Missouri Republican, March 7, 1859.

Missouri Republican, June 6, 1859.

Missouri Republican, June 7, 1859.

Missouri Republican, February 2, 1864.

Missouri Digital Heritage Collection, "Dred Scott Cases, 1846-1857."

Missouri Historical Society Archives, "Rufus Easton (1774-1834) Family Collection, 1796-1897."

Moore Jr., Robert. "A Ray of Hope, Extinguished," *Gateway Heritage* (Winter, 1993-94).

Naden, Corinne J., Rose Blue. *Dred Scott: Person Or Property?* (Oregon City, Oreg.: Marshall Cavendish, 2004).

New York Times, June 8, 1859.

New York Times, November 16, 1859.

New York Times, February 17, 1860.

Nicolay, Helen. "Lincoln's Cabinet," *The Abraham Lincoln Quarterly* (March 1949), 290.

O'Neill, Tim. "150 Years Ago, St. Louis Was Scene of Secession Struggle," *St. Louis Post-Dispatch*, March 6, 2011.

Philips, John F. "Hamilton Rowan Gamble and the Provisional Government of Missouri," *Missouri Historical Review*, vol. 5, no. 1 (October 1910), 1-14.

"Polly Berry," Wikipedia.

Potter, Marguerite. "Hamilton R. Gamble, Missouri's War Governor," *Missouri Historical Review*, vol. 35, no. 1 (October 1940), 25-71.

Primm, James Neal. *Lion in the Valley* 3d ed. (St. Louis: Missouri Historical Society, 1998).

Ruffin, Edmund. *Diary of Edmund Ruffin: The Years of Hope: April, 1861-June, 1863* (Baton Rouge: LSU Press, 1977).

Sacher, John M. *A Perfect War of Politics: Parties, Politicians, and Democracy in Louisiana, 1824-1861* Baton Rouge: LSU Press, 2007).

St. Louis Beacon, February 13, 1830.

St. Louis Globe-Democrat, March 7, 1859.

Scharf, J. Thomas. *History of Saint Louis City and County, From the Earliest Periods to the Present Day: Including Biographical Sketches of Representative Men*, Volume II (Philadelphia: Louis H. Everts & Co., 1883).

Silver, David M. *Lincoln's Supreme Court* (Champaign: University of Illinois Press, 1998).

Shoemaker, Floyd Calvin. *Missouri's Struggle for Statehood from 1804 to 1821* (Jefferson City, Mo.: The Hugh Stephens Printing Company, 1916).

Stevens, Walter B. *St. Louis: The Fourth City, 1764-1922* (St. Louis: S. J. Clarke Publishing, 1911).

Van Ness Bay, William. *Reminiscences of the Bench and Bar of Missouri* (St. Louis: F. H. Thomas and Company, 1878).

Van Ravenswaay, Charles. *St. Louis: An Informal History of the City and Its People, 1764-1865* (St. Louis, Missouri Historical Society Press, 1991).

Williams, Scott K. "Slavery in St. Louis" (2006).

Bloom, William Wirt, and Elizabeth Gaspar Brown. "Territorial Courts and Law: Unifying Factors in the Development of Institutions: Part One, Establishment of a Standardized Judicial System," *Michigan Law Review*, Vol. 61, No. 1 (November, 1962).

Wolff, Chief Justice Michael A. "Race, Law and the Struggle for Equality, Chief Justice Looks at Missouri Law, Politics and the Dred Scott Case." This is a transcript of comments made by the Chief Justice on March 1, 2007, at Washington University.

ABOUT THE AUTHOR

ANTHONY SESTRIC WAS BORN IN JUNE 1940, THE OLDEST SON OF JUDGE ANTON and Marie Sestric, and graduated from "The High School" in 1958. He did his undergraduate work at Georgetown University in Washington, D.C., during which he worked for the Democratic National Committee. Returning to Missouri, he earned his J.D. from the University of Missouri–Columbia in 1965. After graduating, he clerked for Judge Roy Harper, the chief judge for the Eastern District of Missouri before joining his uncle in private practice. He is licensed to practice law in Missouri and Minnesota, the Eastern District of Missouri, the Northern District of Texas, 8th Circuit Court of Appeals, U.S. Tax Court, U.S. Court of Claims, and the United States Supreme Court. At various times, he served as special assistant Missouri attorney general and special assistant circuit attorney in the city of St. Louis. Sestric also served as legal specialist for the Central and Eastern European Legal Initiative to Croatia.

Amongst the various bar associations, he served at the president of the Bar Association of Metropolitan St. Louis, member of the board of governors of the Missouri Bar, chaired the Missouri Bar special committee on Prepaid Legal Services. In the American Bar Association, he served as the state chairman of the Judiciary Committee, circuit chair for the Committee Condemnation, Zoning and Property Use, and was a member of the Standing Committee on Bar Activities and Services. Amongst the awards he earned were the American Bar Association Award of Merit, the Bar Association of Metropolitan St. Louis Award of Merit, and the Legal Services of Eastern Missouri Volunteer Lawyer of the Year.

He has authored papers on various legal topics. He served on various boards of directors, including the St. Louis Airport Commission, the St. Louis Air Pollution Board of Appeals, Full Achievement, Inc., the Legal Aid Society of St. Louis, and St. Elizabeth Academy.

Politically active locally, he served as campaign chair for elections for the president of the Board of Aldermen of St. Louis, U.S. senator, and mayor of the city of St. Louis.